Children in Action

Other titles in this series include:

DORNYEI, Zoltan and THURRELL, Sarah
Conversation and dialogues in action

FRANK, Christine and RINVOLUCRI, Mario
Grammar in action again

GERNGROSS, Gunter and PUCHTA, Herbert
Pictures in action

GOLEBIOWSKA, Aleksandra
Getting students to talk

GRIFFEE, Dale
Songs in action

McKAY, Sandra
Teaching grammar

NUNAN, David
Language teaching methodology

NUNAN, David
Understanding language classrooms

PECK, Antony
Language teachers at work

ROST, Michael
Listening in action

STEMPLESKI, Susan and TOMALIN, Barry
Video in action

STEVICK, Earl
Success with foreign languages

TAYLOR, Linda
Vocabulary in action

TAYLOR, Linda
Teaching and learning vocabulary

WINGATE, Jim
Getting beginners to talk

YALDEN, Janice
The communicative syllabus

Children in Action

A resource book for language teachers of young learners

CARMEN ARGONDIZZO

Prentice Hall

New York   London   Toronto   Sydney   Tokyo   Singapore

PRENTICE HALL INTERNATIONAL ENGLISH LANGUAGE TEACHING

First published 1992 by
Prentice Hall International (UK) Ltd
Campus 400, Maylands Avenue
Hemel Hempstead
Hertfordshire HP2 7EZ
A division of
Simon & Schuster International Group

Typeset in 10½/12½pt Times
by MHL Typesetting Ltd, Coventry

Printed and bound in Great Britain by
Redwood Books, Trowbridge, Wiltshire

Library of Congress Cataloging-in-Publication Data

Argondizzo, Carmen
    Children in action : a resource book for language teachers of
young learners / Carmen Argondizzo.
        p.   cm. — (Language teaching methodology series)
    "English language teaching."
    Includes bibliographical references (p.   ) and index.
    ISBN 0-13-131467-X
    1. Languages, Modern — Study and teaching (Elementary).
2. Activity programs in education. I. Title II. Series.
LB1578.A75   1992
372.6—dc20   91-28503
                                                                      CIP

British Library Cataloguing in Publication Data

Argondizzo, Carmen
    Children in action : A resource book for language
    teachers of young learners. — (Language teaching
    methodology)
    I. Title II. Series
    428.007

    ISBN 0-13-131467-X

2 3 4 5   96 95 94 93

To Michele
and all his friends
who have taught me
what it means to
be a child again

Contents

Preface

With the Language Teaching Methodology Series we have created a special set of books with the *In Action* title. These books are designed to offer teachers material that can be directly used in class. They are resources for action, hence the title. They offer language teachers material which can be adapted with various inputs for their own classroom work. The activities are presented in an accessible and teacher-friendly way, with a clear identification of teacher and learner roles and, above all, they consist of tried and tested tasks. The authors of the books in the *In Action* collection all have considerable practical experience of teaching and of classroom research. It is this combination of principle and practice, available in an easily accessible form for the teacher, which characterises the design of the books. We hope that they will not only help teachers to plan and carry out exciting lessons but also to develop themselves as reflective teachers by suggesting action research that can be done with their own learners.

For many years, teaching foreign and second languages to children was seen as something additional to the normal curriculum provision of school systems. Increasingly, however, this pattern is changing and in many countries, from Australia to Europe, educators have come to recognise the importance of starting foreign-language learning at an early age. Not only does research emphasise the considerable advantages of early learning but also the classroom contexts and objectives of the primary school lend themselves very well to active language-learning methods with their focus on task-based learning within the group. This, of course, characterises the primary-school curriculum and its modes of delivery. In this exciting new contribution to the *In Action* collection in the Language Teaching Methodology Series, Carmen Argondizzo draws on both research and practical experience of this learner group to offer us a systematic and well-illustrated resource book for classroom teaching. *Children in Action* is a fine title and one which captures the exuberance of the teaching activities outlined here. The book is more than a random collection of successful tasks, however; it offers teachers a way of constructing a purposeful learning curriculum for children, one which develops their competence in a systematic way rather than haphazardly presenting them with excitements, however attractive. Such a staged and planned curriculum is all the more important for children because their primary-school experiences will set the foundations for their later learning. Not that the book is to be used only in the structured setting of the school. Many children, after all, are being taught very successfully and imaginatively in non-formal contexts with keen and dedicated teachers. This book is for those teachers also, offering to them ways of designing an informal curriculum for their learners so that when the learners enter the mainstream of formal education they will have already established the bases for language learning and not lost that innocence, that enthusiasm, which characterises children and which, so much, formal teaching often dispels.

The activities are organised with different types of learning task in mind, emphasising a range of language skills and modes of learning. There is great emphasis on learning by doing, echoing here the great theorists, like Dewey and Kilpatrick and Pestalozzi, of practical learning with heart, head and hand. The activities are structured so that they can easily be chained into a sequence for particular learning groups and at each stage teachers are offered opportunities for action research with their own learners so that they can explore the effects of particular activity choice. Carmen Argondizzo offers a very useful teachers' bibliography for further study, and throughout illustrates the tasks she proposes so that they can readily be drawn upon by teachers as models for their own inventions and their own choices.

As General Editor, I hope that the books in this new *In Action* collection will continue the success of the Language Teaching Methodology Series more generally in developing the skills and knowledge of the reflective language teacher in the classroom.

Professor Christopher N. Candlin
General Editor

Acknowledgements

It is my wish to thank those people who have supported me before and throughout the actual writing of this book.

First, I would like to thank Mario Rinvolucri, who encouraged me several times in the past years to start seriously thinking of collecting my ideas and putting them in a book project.

My next thanks go to Seth Lindstronberg, who read my first set of activities, liked them and pushed me to keep on working on my manuscript.

Valerie Cockburn read the manuscript while it was growing and gave me useful comments.

Christopher Candlin, editor of this *In Action* series, read the first brief draft version of the manuscript. He trusted me and 'did not let me go'. I have greatly appreciated his being extremely simple, precise and sensitive when making comments on the activities. He has given me precious suggestions on the overall organisation of the book. Thanks.

Thank you to my son Michele, who, while playing with his friends, taught me interesting games. While observing him performing the games I could easily think how to re-arrange them for the classroom context.

Thank you also to my young Italian and international students who have been the first to try out most of these activities. Their enjoying the activities has encouraged me to use them again.

The idea of writing this book has developed from research on child conversational strategies that I carried out at the Department of Linguistics of Ohio University. During the two years spent studying in this department I was also given the opportunity to teach English to international children in an elementary school. There I gained insights on how to adapt classroom activities suitable to children who speak English as their native language to EFL settings. I feel, therefore, the need to thank Professors Beverly Flanigan, James Coady and Keiko Koda who, by giving me the scholarship, allowed me the possibility of teaching, studying and making research that directed me towards this book.

My friend Nancy Crego has indirectly influenced me towards the shaping of some activities.

Thanks to Western Publishing Co. Inc. for permission to reproduce the drawings on page 130.

C.A.

INTRODUCTION

Introduction

TO TEACHERS

What is in the book?

This is a book from a teacher to teachers who enjoy playing with children and seeing them 'in action'. I wrote it with the aim of enhancing the autonomy and creativity of teachers and learners and with the aim of giving you, the teachers, 'the lively kick' that you often need for your classes.

I selected the activities and adapted them for L2 classroom use from the following:

- Games observed among a group of international children.

- Popular games that children often play.

- School activities used in L2 environments.

And above all from

- Activities I created in my school environment and which were successfully performed by my learners.

The activities focus on four major areas linked to four issues: socialisation, games, content-area language instruction, reading—writing. Each of these four areas has its own specific aim to achieve as I have briefly shown in the table.

Socialisation	Games	Content-area language instruction	Reading—writing
Activities that help the learners get acquainted with the group and with the L2 environment	Activities that promote learning through pleasure	Educational activities aimed at using the L2 as a means to teach subject topics to younger learners	Activities aimed at encouraging learners to read and write for pleasure

Following these areas I have grouped the activities into five sections:

1. 'Get together' activities.

2. Games children like to play.

3. Educational activities (including Class routines, Art, Music, Physical Education, Maths and Culture).

4. Time for reading.

5. Time for writing.

A final brief section is devoted to Time for rewards.

In the activities I have tried to take into account some relevant and common stages of child L2 development and some of the major discourse strategies that children apply in conversational contexts and play settings (silence, nonsense language, code-switching, borrowings). I have also tried to recreate classroom activities that are often used in English-speaking countries (e.g. 'Show and tell') and popular games that children like to play (e.g. 'The ring', 'Hopscotch', 'Ring-a-ring-a-rosy'). I was encouraged to do this since I believe that a school environment favourable to second-language learning should provide help in building up the skills that children need to acquire through exposure to the L2 in naturalistic and relaxed contexts. Therefore, we should *create a classroom environment* which promotes motivation ('I am learning a language — why am I learning it?'); we should *adopt a learner-centred approach* which encourages major focus on the learners' personalities, individual abilities and interests; and we should *introduce topics, language and situations* relevant to the age of the children (what children talk about, what language expressions they use to carry out their conversation, in what play settings they enjoy being engaged, what content-area topics they enjoy learning first).

Whom is the book for?

The book is for those of you who teach young learners English as a foreign or as a second language.

The activities are suitable for multilingual and monolingual groups. The level of the activities covers a range from complete beginners to intermediate and advanced learners.

Aim of the book: bridging the gap between process strategies in child L2 acquisition and the FL classroom

Child process strategies

A period of silence, the use of meaningful imitation and, later on, the use of creative speech are common features of the *developmental process* of language acquisition in children who are exposed to a second language in an English-speaking country.

During this process *conversational strategies* such as *silence, repetition, pseudo-language* (string of nonsense syllables) and *restricted two-way communication* (the child responds orally to the interactor but does not use the target language — he uses, instead, the first language or nonverbal responses) are often adopted by children.

Moreover, the early acquisition of *formulaic expressions* that children use as unanalysed chunks of language and, at later stages, the use of *telegraphese* (single-word or two-word utterances) lead the children to creative speech.

Borrowings are also commonly used by children acquiring a second language. They are considered a normal conversational strategy that bilinguals use in order to convey meaning. They provide an additional linguistic resource on which bilingual children may draw to enhance their communication.

In the language classroom

Conversational strategies such as the ones mentioned above may sound to you like common features among children acquiring the L2 in an English-speaking country. However, it is my intention to offer you activities that recall some of these strategies. My major aim is, in fact, to encourage the recreation of naturalistic settings within the classroom.

Silent games like 'Replay', 'Stop when you hear . . .', 'The ball' do not necessarily require the children to speak. What is relevant here is that they understand the language input provided by you and react to it.

In 'Rush the sentence' you will give the children the opportunity to learn and practise daily formulaic expressions through a game.

The Language Play set of games will teach children the language while they play with its sounds. You will find out how pre-school and school children enjoy making up nonsense language and nonsense sounds. The activities will also help them get familiar with 'strange' sounds and become aware of the concept of foreign language.

In 'I say, you repeat' the children produce repetition that is meaningful because their task is to show that they are aware of being (or feeling) familiar with the language.

In the 'L2 "borrowing" game' you will give the children the chance to produce L2 words and use them within appropriate contexts even before they are able to perform fully in the second language at the sentence level.

Playing in the language classroom

During their play-time children often and spontaneously begin object play, fantasy play and sociodramatic play. Object play is reality-based and involves manipulation of and reference to the objects themselves. Fantasy play refers to episodes that evoke a fantastic or imaginative context and involves object substitution or the invocation of imaginary objects. Similar to this is dramatic play which consists of a make-believe world in which children engage and invite others to participate.

In the activities I have included examples of *object play* (I called it here 'realistic play'), *fantasy play*, *sociodramatic play* and *let's pretend*. The play settings that I have chosen for the book are among the popular ones that children engage in. Moreover, some of them ('Our little people' and 'The micro-cities') involves the use of toys that children enjoy a lot or toys imaginatively created by the children. However, you are free to expand the activities proposed by changing the themes according to what your learners enjoy better.

With the set of games that include 'Show and tell', 'Ring-a-ring-a-rosy', 'Races', '1–2–3–4 ... FREEZE!', 'Hopscotch','Chase and catch', 'Who's got the ring?', 'A day in the life of ...', 'Halloween', 'Be mine ... on Valentine's Day', my intention was to involve the children in international games and activities that I have adapted for classroom use. The children get high motivation, in fact, from performing an activity just because they know that it is something done by other children in another part of the world. This will give them the chance to 'taste' a little part of the foreign culture.

Content-area language instruction: building up motivation in the FL learner

Most children who start FL instruction do not have autonomous motivation to learn a foreign language. Motivation is often encouraged by the families who create an interest towards the new language. This motivation is reinforced at school by the teachers who regularly create curiosity about the different styles of life and different habits of the people who speak the foreign language. The aim of this is to make the children aware of the existence of different cultures and make them accept the diversities in social behaviours that may be considered inappropriate at times by learners.

However, teachers may also encourage motivation by planning content-area language activities that will build up knowledge of topics covered in other school subjects through the use of the L2. This will promote the introduction of language activities that are planned across subjects and may help those who have to plan syllabuses across the school curriculum. Language instruction is thus not seen as an end in itself but as a means to the exploitation of themes linked with other subject areas.

The subjects that I have involved in the section on Educational Activities are art, music, physical education (PE), maths, culture. The activities at times introduce a specific topic as in 'Colour game: primary and secondary colours' (art), 'Search for the English word' (PE), 'Shape in, shape out' (maths), 'Halloween' (culture). At times they are not specifically relevant at the content level but are more generally linked with the subject areas, as in 'Rap the words' (music: fun while being musical), 'The hungriest poster' (art: free drawing) and 'Listen and move' (PE: developing motor skills). Activities of this kind are endless. I hope I have provided for you some basic examples that you may use as a starting point for further activities creatively planned by yourself.

How to use the book

The book provides ready-planned material for use in class. Some of the activities have simple texts ready to be photocopied and they often involve simple practical tasks which aim to encourage creativity and lively reactions on the side of your learners.

The activities do not build language skills systematically. Therefore, you do not need to use the activities in sequence but you can select them according to the particular needs of your learners during the school year and integrate them into the material in the coursebook (if you have one). However, the section **Links** that you find in the description of the activities indicate how each activity can be chained and connected with others in the book. This will create the possibility for some curricular progression.

The section **Variations** that you find in many activities shows how the activity in question could be extended if you are dealing with faster or slower learners.

The section **Teacher's diary** encourages you to do some simple action research within your class, discovering how your students did the tasks, what kind of results emerged and how the children seemed to be learning.

In this section you will be encouraged to answer questions like the following:

How did the children perform in this activity? Which step of the activity did the children enjoy best? Was it easy to organise the activity? Could the children remember the language expressions easily? etc.

Most of the times you will need to look for the answers together with your students. This should help you become more aware of some details of your students' learning in progress. At the same time, this should help the children become aware of what they do in class, why and how they do it. It will be rewarding for them to be participants and feel 'in action' also in this final section.

Classroom management: getting organised for the activities

The scheme that you find at the beginning of each activity aims to make you aware of what you need to know before planning an activity and what organisation is necessary in order to perform an activity. The scheme includes headings related to the following three general areas:

1. *Language* involved

    Topic
    Activity type
    Language
    Background knowledge
    Purpose

2. *Organisation* behind the activity

    Time
    Classroom setting
    Materials

3. Suitable *group*

    Age
    Level

- **Topic** mentions what themes will be covered during the activity.

- **Activity type** highlights the major action the children will perform.

- **Language** includes grammar exponents and/or words used in the activity.

- **Background knowledge** explains the language knowledge you expect the children to have in order to be able to perform the activity successfully.

- **Time** gives the approximate length of time that you expect the activity to last.

- **Classroom setting** gives the suggested settings for the activity. Changes of settings within the same activity and from one activity to another are of great importance in keeping the attention of the children alive. See which settings your children like best and use them as often as you can (e.g. children often love sitting in a circle on the floor).

- **Materials** informs about 'what' is needed in order to perform the activity.

- **Purpose** gives the communicative and cognitive objectives that you expect the children to achieve.

- **Age** and **Level** give the approximate age and level of English proficiency that the children should have to perform the activity.

Order vs chaos

Many activities suggested in this book may sound to you too hard to manage with children and may discourage you from performing them for fear of creating a chaotic classroom environment. To overcome this feeling I suggest you have a clear idea of the scheme presented above and provided for you in the description of each activity before organising your class. Moreover, it will be necessary to be fully aware of the objectives that you want the children to achieve. Even an apparently *chaotic* class will then have an *ordered* organisational framework that will allow you to do the activities without difficulty and to get the desired results.

L1 vs L2: the role of code-switching and borrowings

The labels L1 and L2 suggest to you when it is more appropriate to speak one or the other language. While performing the practical tasks requested in several activities, monolingual groups will naturally create examples of borrowings and code-switching from the L1 into the L2.

This should not be seen as inappropriate. It is, instead, spontaneous language production that shows the ability of the learners to create their own structures during a stage in which they are not yet fully fluent in using the L2. Teachers should, therefore, become sensitive enough to understand when L1 is needed (e.g. when giving instructions, when talking about the activities) as opposed to L2 (e.g. when performing the activities).

Reading and writing: when do we start?

Introduce reading and writing instruction in the L2 as soon as you realise that the children are ready and interested in seeing the written forms of the language. Reading, in particular, seems to develop more rapidly than speaking. It is not uncommon, in fact, for non-native speakers of English to understand what they read but not be able to retell it orally in English. Reading need not, therefore, follow oral development but may be parallel to it and contribute to general language control.

The reading activities that I am proposing here focus on areas that children need to develop and that may be of interest to them:

- *Vocabulary expansion*
  This section stresses the importance of introducing new words in context during the first stages of child language learning. This aims at helping the learners begin the production of one- and two-word utterances as children do when acquiring their mother tongue.

- *Accuracy and cohesiveness*
  This section helps the children become aware of accuracy and cohesiveness at the sentence level as in 'The "what, when, where, how" game' and discourse level — e.g. daily exchanges as in 'Choose what to say'.

- *Reading aloud*
  This section focuses on pronunciation and intonation practice linked with meaning.

- *Reading for pleasure (extensive reading)*
  This section stresses the importance of extensive reading.

- *Reading aloud to children*
  In this section listening and reading skills are integrated.

Select a large number of native-speaker books suitable to the age and interest of your students. Use them for activities like 'Jigsaw story' or types of activity such as 'Reading for pleasure' or 'Reading aloud to children'. This will encourage you to expose the children to a different language context while making this context accessible through an easy and enjoyable activity.

Integrating reading and writing skills

It has often been suggested that we should encourage our learners to relate what they read to their own world of knowledge and experience; that is, start from the text to get to the learners' experience.

Following a similar approach, the activity 'Your story, my writing' encourages the children to tell a short story to the teacher (in the L1 in our FL settings). The teacher writes down the story in the L2. This will then be ready to be read by the whole class. This technique often gives good results since the students will be motivated to read their stories to see how they 'sound' in the L2. By using this technique you will start from the learners' experience to get to a text written by you but created by the children. By doing so you will give your children practice in reading and writing skills while stimulating their creativity.

The English corner and the English walls

It is always very useful to organise a corner where all 'the English stuff' is stored or where the various posters made up during the school year can be stored. Call it the 'English corner' and use it to display books, magazines, cartoons, brochures, drawings, flashcards that you used in class or will use. Put an English bulletin board there, where children can hang up their favourite wall-charts or cards. Encourage the children to feel responsible about it and encourage them, in turn, to keep it in order and add new material if they wish to. Obviously, this will be hard if you teach several classes, but you can manage easily if you have only one or two groups.

Choose two walls in the classroom, use these 'English walls' as often as you can. Display as much as you can on them and change the posters displayed from time to time. This will be fun for the children and will make the classroom environment lively. The posters displayed will help the children recall the activities performed more easily and the language input introduced through them. Also use the materials displayed on the walls as a resource for reviewing activities.

Children's errors: teachers' attitude

Teachers have often considered errors as the unpleasant part of the language class. They would feel happy if their learners could produce perfect language from the very first days. This is, however, impossible. Errors can be produced because of the following:

- Interference from the mother tongue, for example:

    The my book as opposed to *my book* for Italian learners.

- Interference within the same language that causes overgeneralisation

    e.g. *I want not* as an overgeneralisation of *I am not*.

- Developmental stages of acquisition

    e.g. developmental errors linked to the process of acquisition that create examples of interlanguage as in *I no want water*.

We should try to keep in mind, however, that errors are often evidence of a productive phase that children go through. During this phase the children's ability to create language is the basic positive step that confirms their learning in process.

Some correction techniques

We still need to correct, however, but the question is how best to do it. We have to be, therefore, sensitive enough to become aware of what, when and how errors have to be corrected. The following techniques are often useful with young learners:

1. *Peer correction*
    When a child or a group of children are performing an activity, tell the other children that they are going to be the 'teachers'. Therefore, they will have to make the corrections. You will find out that peers are often more precise than teachers! And they will also have lots of fun!

2. *Use your fingers*
    Be silent and use your fingers to help them understand which part of the sentence was wrong; for example: *I **have** eight years old*. Touch your thumb — that stands for *I* — and nod to mean 'correct'; touch your middle finger — that stands for *eight* — and nod to mean 'correct'; touch your pointer — that stands for *have* — and show with your head and face expression that you disagree; for example, move your head from right to left.

3. *Clap and use your lips*
    Clap when you hear the mistake and say the correct form with your lips until the children understand it.

4. *Listen, note down and say*
    Observe the children while they are performing an activity, listen to what they produce, note down errors that really 'bother' you. Report the errors to the children when the activity is over. Together with your 'error report', also make comments on general performance; for example, 'You sounded self-confident'; 'You looked shy'; 'Your pronunciation was correct'; 'It seemed you were enjoying yourself'; etc.

My message to you is, therefore, the following: 'Correction? Yes, but do it at the appropriate time, kindly and only when it's significant!'

Role of rewards

Rewards play an important role in the motivation and school development of younger learners. Give them a reward as often as you can. Use the *Time for Rewards* section whenever you have the chance. Ask the children to collect their rewards, show them at home as a sign of their progress and check how many they have clocked up at the end of a term and at the end of the school year. The use of the rewards suggested in this book will also help them enrich their knowledge of reward expressions.
  Good luck!

Useful references

If you wish to get more information about the field of teaching children ESL/EFL you may find some of the books listed below of interest to you. I have divided the list of suggested titles into four different sets: 'Activities', 'Materials', 'Field research', 'Theoretical background'. If you wish to concentrate on practical ideas you may find it useful to look through the two sets of 'Activities' and 'Materials'. If you are willing to get deeper insights into children's second-language acquisition look through the suggestions given in the 'Field research' and 'Theoretical background' sets. The list is obviously not exhaustive of books available in this field. (The titles are listed alphabetically by author.)

Activities

In the books listed below you will be introduced to activities and games suitable for pre-school and school children. Some of these books describe activities designed for or played by children who are English native speakers. You will find out, however, how most activities are easily adaptable to English-language classrooms. These kinds of activity give school children the opportunity to expand their language experience through fun and play.

Michele and Craig Borba, *Self-Esteem: A classroom affair*, Harper and Row, 1982.
K. Godman *et al.*, *Reading in the Bilingual Classroom: Literacy and biliteracy*, National Clearinghouse for Bilingual Education, 1979.
Cristina Laris, *EFL/ESL Poems and Fingerplays*, Scott Foresman, 1987.
Jean Marzollo and Janice Lloyd, *How to Help Children Learn through Play*, Scholastic, 1973.
Iona and Peter Opie, *Children's Games of Street and Playground*, Oxford University Press, 1984.
Iona and Peter Opie, *The Lore and Language of School Children*, Oxford University Press, 1987.
Schools Council, *Scope: An introductory course for immigrant children*, Teachers' Book, Longman, 1969.
Dorothy G. and Jerome L. Singer, *Make Believe: Games and activities to foster imaginative play in young children*, Scott Foresman, 1985.

Materials

This set lists books that are written for children who speak English as their first language. Here, again, by looking through these books you will easily discover how much you can do with them in your language classroom. They also help you develop further ideas for creative activities. Books of this kind and ESL/EFL readers are often available in the children's section of ESL/EFL bookshops in major cities.

Stan and Jan Berenstain, *The Berenstain Bears' Nursery Tales*, Random House, 1973.
Stan and Jan Berenstain, *The Berenstain Bears' and the Messy Room*, Random House, 1983.
Michael and Karen Bond, *Paddington's Clock Book*, Rand McNally, 1986.

Norman Bridwell, *Clifford the Big Red Dog*, Scholastic, 1985.
Dr Seuss, *Hop on Pop*, Beginner Books, 1963.
Karen Gundetsheimer, *Happy Winter*, Harper and Row, 1982.
Roger Hargreaves, *Mr Men Books*, Happiness Books, 1972.
K.M. Kostyal, *Animals at Play*, National Geographic Society, 1988.
Mercer Mayer, *All by Myself*, Western, 1983.
My First Book of Words, Western, 1980.
Beatrix Potter, *The Tale of Peter Rabbit*, Scholastic, 1986.

Field research

The following articles and books are a sample of conversational-analysis research on
children. Reading articles of this kind will give you examples of how field work in
child language development — both L1 and L2 — is carried out and what kind of
insights are developed from this research.

M.A. Evans, 'Play beyond play', in L. Galda and A. Pellegrini (eds), 1985.
L. Galda and A. Pellegrini (eds), *Play, Language and Stories: The development of
    children's literate behavior*, Ablex, 1985.
D. Larsen-Freeman (ed.), *Discourse Analysis in Second Language Research*, Newbury
    House, 1980.
S. Peck, 'Language play in child second language acquisition', in D. Larsen-Freeman
    (ed.), 1980.
J. Sachs, J. Goldman and C. Chaille, 'Narratives in preschoolers' sociodramatic play:
    the role of knowledge and communicative competence', in L. Galda and
    A. Pellegrini (eds), 1985.

Theoretical background

The following books — or sections of them — give a theoretical view on major features
of child's language acquisition. The ones on second-language acquisition, in particular,
cover topics like the effects of motivation, environment, age and personality on second-
language development.

H.H. Clark and E. Clark, *Psychology and Language: An introduction to psycho-
    linguistics*, Harcourt Brace Jovanovich, 1977.
M.A.K. Halliday, *Learning How to Mean: Explorations in the development of language*,
    Edward Arnold, 1975.
E. Hatch, *Psycholinguistics: A second language perspective*, Newbury House, 1983.
B. McLaughlin, *Second Language Acquisition in Childhood*, 2 vols, Lawrence Erlbaum,
    1984.

SECTION I

'GET TOGETHER'
ACTIVITIES

1 Replay

Topic	Sports (or any other chosen by you)
Activity type	Silent answer game
Language	Words related to the topic
Time	20−25 minutes
Classroom setting	Children standing and moving around the classroom
Materials	A set of pictures of popular sports
Age	6 and above
Level	Beginner and elementary
Purpose	Expanding vocabulary related to sports; providing words related to a familiar language context

Preparation

Prepare a set of flashcards with pictures of popular sports.

In class

1. **(In L1)** Explain to the children what 'replay' is. Ask if they have ever seen 'replay' on the television when watching sports like soccer, baseball, gymnastics. Tell them that the purpose of the slow motion of 'replay' is to show the details of an action.

2. **(In L2)** Show the pictures to the children. Tell them the names of the sports shown in the pictures.

3. Divide the children into pairs or small groups. Say:

   Now we play 'Replay'.

Call a group and ask them to mime the sport that you are going to mention. Say the name of a sport — without showing the picture this time. The children in the group mime actions of the sport with slow motions. The other children say if they have 'replayed' the appropriate sport.

Variations

Call a group and whisper the name of a sport to them. The children in the group mime actions of the sport with slow motions. The children in the other group guess the name of the sport.

Links

You may link this activity with: **Search for the English word (57).**

Teacher's diary

Were the children able to 'replay' the actions? Did they enjoy it? Was it easy for them to remember the names of the sports?

---

2 Stop when you hear . . .

Topic	Any chosen by you
Activity type	Silent answer game
Language	Words related to the topic
Background knowledge	The children should know the set of words that you choose for the activity
Time	20–25 minutes
Classroom setting	Children in a circle around the classroom
Materials	A list of words
Age	6–12
Level	Elementary
Purpose	Recognising familiar words mentioned within an unfamiliar language context

Preparation

1. Prepare a list of words that the children have never come across. Along with these items list also a small set of words that are familiar to the children (e.g. a set of words related to colours — yellow, blue, red, etc.).

In class

Tell the children that you are going to say some words to them. When they hear words related to 'colours' they have to sit down.

Say:

> Stand up everybody and march in a circle.

Let them march for a little while. Then start saying your list of words. Check if the children sit on the floor when they hear the first word related to the familiar set. Say:

> OK. Everybody up now. Let's march again.

Continue with your list until all the familiar words have been recognised.

Variations

Make it easier

If the children are just starting the L2 instruction, you can just call their names instead of the familiar set of words. This time the game ends when all the children have been called and all are sitting down.

Make it difficult

If the children know a lot of words in English, say the names of 'green (or any other colour you choose) things' as they march. Every time they hear something 'green', they sit down; e.g. 'banana, water, stop sign, grass (they sit), a blueberry, the sun, an egg, a big green tree (they sit), an orange, a red hen, the sky, an alligator (they sit), a turtle, a goldfish', etc.

Links

You may link this activity with: **A birthday gift (41)**; **The dictionary poster (42)**; **Colour game: primary and secondary colours (47)**.

Teacher's diary

Were the children able to recognise the familiar words? If you have played the section 'Variations' were they able to associate the 'things' with the 'colour'? Did they enjoy the game?

---

3 The ball

Topic	Identities
Activity type	Silent answer game
Language	'I'm'
Time	10—20 minutes
Classroom setting	Children standing or sitting in a circle on the floor
Materials	A ball
Age	6 and above
Level	Beginner and above
Purpose	Socialising

Preparation

Bring a ball (any kind) to class.

In class

1. Arrange the children in a circle, possibly sitting on the floor. Sit in the circle as a member of it. Create a quiet atmosphere. Get the ball out of your bag, show it to the children and throw it to a child. Invite the child — with a gesture — to do the same with another child. This goes on in silence for a few minutes, with only some giggling of the more lively children.

2. Get the ball, say your name and throw it to a child. The child says his name and throws the ball to someone else.

3. When the round has been completed, get the ball again, say:

    I'm [+ your name]

and throw the ball. The child who gets it does the same or nods to show comprehension and throws the ball. Have another round. Get the ball again, say:

> I'm [+ your name]

make a pause, then say:

> I'm a teacher.

Throw the ball to a child you expect to be able to react to your stimulus. The child repeats the phrases and says:

> I'm [+ name]. I'm a student.

If nobody knows the word 'student' whisper it until someone understands it.

4. Continue in the same way with 'age'. But first count a few of them to get to the children's age; for example, if the children are six years old, walk around counting the first six children to help them understand what number-word they need to produce. Then say:

> I'm [+ your name].
> I'm a teacher.
> I'm [make a gesture meaning 'My goodness, too old?'] thirty-eight.

Throw the ball and expect the children to produce

> I'm [+ name]. I'm a student. I'm six.

5. **(In L1)** When the game is over, ask the children what they think they have said during the activity.

Variations

Make it difficult

Add a new sentence each round (e.g. 'I like ...', 'I don't like ...', 'My favourite ...', 'The thing I like best is ...') until the children produce a full set of personal information. When you add a new, more difficult sentence, take into account what language your students already know.

Links

You may link this activity with: **Rush the sentence (4)**; **Name cards (9)**.

4 Rush the sentence

Topic	Common formulaic expressions
Activity type	Using everyday expressions
Language	Expressions related to the topic
Time	20–25 minutes
Classroom setting	Children sitting in a circle on the floor
Materials	A small ball
Age	6–13
Level	Beginner–intermediate
Purpose	Getting familiar with the meaning and pronunciation of formulaic expressions

Preparation

Prepare a list of common formulaic expressions that you want to introduce to the children; for example:

Hello! Hi!
How are you doing?
Good morning. Goodbye. See you.
My name's _____. What's your name?
How are you? Fine, thanks.
I'm seven. How old are you?
Thank you. Welcome.

In class

Part 1

1. Arrange the children in a circle sitting on the floor. Get the ball and sit among

the children as a member of the group. Throw the ball to one child. Keep silent. The child gets the ball and throws it to someone else still keeping silent. After a few minutes of silent game, get the ball again, say the first expression and throw the ball to a child. She gets it, repeats the expression and throws the ball to another peer. This continues until you get the ball again. Say the second expression and continue the game. Stop when you have introduced the first three or four expressions.

2. Ask the children what they think they have been saying so far. Suggest a few communicative functions that may help them become aware of the language they are just learning to use; for example:

> **(In L1)** You have greeted your friends by saying . . .
> You have said your name.
> You have asked their names.
> You have thanked . . .

Part 2

3. Check if the children are sitting close enough around the circle. Then start the 'rush the sentence' game. Whisper one of the expressions the children have just learned in the ear of the one sitting on your right. He listens to you, turns towards the peer sitting on his right and repeats the expression. This goes on around the circle with the children repeating one after the other in the ear of the child sitting next. Do it as fast as possible, avoiding interruptions. End the 'round' only when all the children have said the expression without making mistakes (do not expect perfection, though!).

Change expression and continue the game until the children enjoy it and — possibly — until you have completed the list of formulaic expressions planned for the day.

Variations

Make it difficult

Instead of the set of formulaic expressions, have a short story to tell to the children. Follow step 3. Begin the 'rush the sentence' rounds. Whisper a sentence of the story each round. When you finish the story and the rounds, ask the children to retell the story aloud this time.

Links

You may link this activity with: **The ball (3)**; **Gestures (5)**; **I say, you repeat (20)**; **Choose what to say (69)**; **Jigsaw story (71)**.

5 Gestures

Topic	Gestures
Activity type	Silent answer game
Language	Expressions related to the topic
Background knowledge	The children should already be familiar with the expressions listed below
Time	30–40 minutes
Classroom setting	Any
Materials	A set of flashcards with the expressions listed below written on them
Age	7 and above
Level	Elementary and intermediate
Purpose	Becoming aware of the importance of body language; increasing the knowledge of L2 expressions that can be said through gestures

Preparation

Make a list of expressions that the children already know and that can be 'said' using gestures. Write them on flashcards.

In class

1. Introduce the children to the concept of 'body language'. Tell them to show and explain the meaning of the most common gestures that they usually make in their mother tongue. Inform them that gestures change from one country to another although the meaning can be the same. Give some examples that you know.

2. Get the flashcards. Read the expressions aloud and ask the children — if they understand the meaning — to make the gestures they think are appropriate for each expression.

3. Divide the children into two groups. Call one group 'gesture' and the other group 'expression'. Stick the flashcards on the wall. The 'gesture' group chooses a card — without picking it up — and one of them makes the appropriate gesture. The 'expression' group says what expression the gesture means by reading the appropriate card. Switch roles between the two groups.

The following are simple expressions that can be 'said' through body language. Use these expressions for this activity. Change them or add others according to the background knowledge that the children in your classroom have. Do not use these expressions in just one lesson if you think too many expressions may confuse your students.

Expressions	Gestures*
Hello	wave
Goodbye	wave
It's cold	put arms round shoulders
It's hot	fan your face with hands
No!	move your head from left to right
Don't do it again!	move index finger up and down
Come here	move index finger towards you
Me!	put your hand up
Me?	touch your chest
OK	make an 'o' with index finger and thumb
I don't understand	pull shoulders up, spread arms apart
You're stupid	stick your tongue out
Shhhhh	put index finger in front of your mouth
Victory	make a V with your index finger and middle finger
Thank you	bend your head gently
Stop	put your hand up with fingers spread out
I don't know	pull your shoulders up
Be quiet	move your hand up and down gently
Crazy!	touch your forehead with index finger
I'm tired	yawn or touch your eyes pressing them gently
Go away!	move index finger from your chest away from your body
Stand up!	raise your hand slightly (palm up)
Sit down	your hand goes slightly down (palm down)

*Be careful, though, gestures are culture bound and differ from one place to another, e.g.

Goodbye: wave hand right to left (Italian)   wave hand up and down (American)

Make the children aware of it.

Variations

Make it difficult

Hide the flashcards. The children who belong to the 'expression' group have to say the expressions without having the chance to read them.

Links

You may link this activity with: **Rush the sentence (4)**.

Teacher's diary

Did the children understand the concept of body language? Did they already know some gestures? Do they use some? Was it easy for them to match 'gestures' with expressions in the foreign/second language?

6 Follow the leader

Activity type	Socialising
Language	'Follow', 'change', 'leader'
Time	15–20 minutes
Classroom setting	Children playing around the classroom
Materials	A card that says 'LEADER' in large letters
Age	6–11
Level	Beginner and elementary
Purpose	Giving children the chance to have a leading role; understanding simple directions

In class

Say:

> Stand in a row ... one after the other. Put your arms on the shoulders of the child standing in front of you.

Make gestures to help the children understand the meaning of your instructions. Hang the card that says 'LEADER' around the neck of the first child. Say:

> Follow the leader.

The leader moves around and the other children follow him as if they were a 'train'. Let them do this for a little while. Then say:

> Change the LEADER.

Pick up the card and put it around the neck of another child. Say:

> Follow the LEADER.

This child goes first and keeps on leading the train around the classroom.

Continue until all the children have had the chance to be leaders at least once.

Variations

Make it difficult

While the children are moving around, give them directions like 'Go to the right', 'Go to the left', 'Go straight', 'Stop', etc. or 'Let's go to the right', 'Let's all go to the left now', etc. Then ask the leaders to give directions like those above.

Links

You may link this activity with: **The crazy train (7)**; **The micro-cities (26)**; **1−2−3−4 ... FREEZE! (33)**.

Teacher's diary

Did the children enjoy the activity? Did they enjoy being leaders? Did they understand your directions easily? Were they able to give the directions? How long did it take them to learn how to give the directions?

---

7 The crazy train

Activity type   Socialising

Language   'Slowly', 'fast', 'faster', 'train', 'fall down'

Time   15−20 minutes

Classroom setting   Children playing around the classroom or in the playground

Age   6−11

Level   Beginner and elementary

Purpose   Getting familiar with words involved in simple directions

In class

Say:

> Let's play 'choo-choo train'.

Arrange the children as if they were a long train: one child standing behind another. Each child keeps his arms on the shoulders of the one standing in front.

While the children move around give rhythm to their motions by saying:

> Go slowly choo-choo train, go slowly choo-choo train.

Let them say: 'Choo-choo train, choo-choo train, choo-choo train' while they are moving around.

Speed up the rhythm little by little and say:

> Go faster choo-choo train, go faster choo-choo train, go faster choo-choo train.

Say it faster and faster. The children speed up their motion and say: 'Choo-choo train, choo-choo train' faster, too. Say:

> ... until the train falls down!

The children fall on the floor and lie there for a few moments. Then the game starts again.

When the children get ready for production, let them, in turn, take your role and give the commands to the train.

Variations

Make it difficult

While the train is moving around give directions to the children like: 'Go to the right choo-choo train', 'Go to the left', 'Go straight', 'Stop', etc. Ask the children to give commands like those above.

Links

You may link this activity with: **Follow the leader (6)**; **Ring-a-ring-a-rosy (8)**; **The micro-cities (26)**; **Chase and catch (29)**.

Teacher's diary

Did the children understand your commands easily? Were they able to give the commands? How long did it take them to learn how to give the commands? Did they enjoy falling down?

8 Ring-a-ring-a-rosy

Activity type	Socialising
Language	'Ring around', 'fall down'
Time	15–20 minutes
Classroom setting	Children playing around the classroom or in the playground
Age	6–7
Level	Beginner
Purpose	Getting familiar with the sounds and words involved in the rhyme

In class

1. Say:

    Let's play ring-a-ring-a-rosy.

    Arrange the children in a circle, and say:

    Hold hands.

    Make gestures to make the meaning of the commands clear. Move around together with the children and sing:

    Ring-a-ring-a-rosy,
    A pocket full of posies
    A-tish-oo, a-tish-oo
    We all fall down.

    Fall down together with the children. Repeat it several times, until the children enjoy it. Ask them to repeat the rhyme after you when they are ready to do it.

2. Focus on the new words by asking the children to tell the meaning of 'ring', 'rosy' and 'fall down'. The children do the appropriate motions or translate into their L1.

Variations

Make it difficult

Write the following on the blackboard:

_____-a-_____-a-_____,
A pocket full of posies
A-tish-oo, a-tish-oo
We all _____ _____.

ring, rosy, fall down, ring

Ask the children to read the rhyme and fill in the blanks with the appropriate words.

Links

You may link this activity with: **The crazy train (7)**; **Shape in, shape out (58)**; **Make a poem (85)**.

Teacher's diary

Did the children remember the rhyme easily? What other rhymes can you use for this activity? How about rhymes made up by the children?

9 Name cards

Topic	Names
Activity type	Socialising
Time	10 minutes
Age	6 and above
Level	Beginner and above
Purpose	Socialising, getting to know the children's names

In class

1. Ask the children to prepare a card with their names written on it in large letters. The children decorate the card and put it on the desk visible to the teacher. Ask them to show the cards for a week or so until you have learned all the children's names.

2. After a few days, tell the children to cover the cards and play the 'name game': you have to call out the names of all the children. Do it when you are sure that you can remember all their names.

    This simple activity has always worked as an opportunity for each child to feel at the centre of the teacher's attention. It also helps you learn the children's names faster.

Variations

Collect the name cards. Pick up one, read the name and give it to the appropriate child. Go on until you have given back all the cards.

Links

You may link this activity with: **Stop when you hear ... (2)**; **The ball (3)**.

10 The 'ME' sign-board

Topic	Turn-taking
Activity type	Socialising
Language	'Me'
Time	10–15 minutes
Classroom setting	Any
Materials	A sign-board, crayons, a short stick
Age	6–11
Level	Beginner
Purpose	Getting aware of taking turns at talking

Preparation

Tell the children to bring a paste-board (any shape) and a stick.

In class

Tell the children to write a big 'ME' on their paste-board. Let them colour the board the way they like. Then they paste the board on to the stick.

Tell them they will use this sign-board every time they want to take turns at speaking during the 'quiet' activities. The 'ME' sign-board helps to calm down especially those noisier classes where a large group of children want to talk at the same time. With this activity you help them to become aware of 'turn taking' in speaking. You will also help the 'shy' children to have their chance to speak, rather than be excluded from participating by the extroverts.

Variations

Make it difficult

Prepare a list of classroom rules. Include the following:

- Take turns when you want to speak.

- Put your hand up when you want to speak.

- Put up your 'ME' sign-board when you want to speak.

Links

You may link this activity with: **Date, weather, time, the register (35).**

Teacher's diary

Do the children remember to use the 'ME' sign-board regularly? Did this help to build up 'turn-taking' rules?

---

11   Nicknames

Topic	Nicknames
Activity type	Socialising
Language	'Miss', 'Mr', words related to the topic
Time	30—40 minutes
Classroom setting	Any
Materials	A large sheet of paper, photographs of the children, a list of nicknames
Age	8 and above
Level	Elementary—intermediate
Purpose	Becoming aware of children's personalities; increasing vocabulary

Preparation

Prepare a list of 'nicknames' that may be appropriate for the children in your classroom.

Ask the children to bring a photo of themselves or use a group photograph if you have one.

Activity

1. Ask the children to think of a special 'something' about their peers. Give them a short time to do that and provide them with some hints (L1 admitted); for example:

    Who is the one who always laughs?
    Who is the one who always talks?
    Who is the shy one?
    Who is the naughty one?

Who is arrogant?
Who is nervous?
etc.

Go to the blackboard and elicit comments (L1 still admitted) from them; for example:

Maria always talks.
Giovanni always fights.
etc.

While the children make their comments in their mother tongue, write on the blackboard at random the appropriate translation for the 'nicknames'; for example:

Maria always talks → Miss Talky Talky
Giovanni always fights → Mr Fight

When the blackboard is full with nicknames, read these names to the children.

- Can they recall whom each name refers to?
  (Write their names under or next to each nickname while they give their answers.)

- Do they understand the meaning of each nickname?
  (If not, give them help with gestures or translating into the L1.)

- Do they all agree on each nickname?
  (If not, make changes following their suggestions.)

- Can they read the nicknames and pronounce them correctly?
  (Help them do it.)

Now cover the blackboard or turn it around in order to hide the nicknames.

- Can each of them recall his own nickname now?

- Can they remember their classmates' nicknames?

Elicit answers, then uncover the blackboard (or turn it back) for checking.

2. Hang the sheet of paper on the wall and write 'Our nicknames' at the top. Invite the children to stick their photos on it. Then they write their nicknames next to each photo.
    Suggested nicknames that can be used in the classroom:

Miss Jealous, Mr Nervous, Miss Aggressive, Mr Strong, Miss Happy, Mr Fuss, Mr Clean, Mr Tidy, Mr Messy, Mr Nickname (someone who gives nicknames to everyone in the classroom), Mr Wise, Mr Chubby, Miss Lazy, Mr Sleepy, Miss Miss (someone who takes care of her person too much),

Mr Funny, Miss Lively, Mr Small, Miss Ginger (someone with red hair), Mr Quiet, Miss Clever, Mr Hair, Miss Pessimist, Mr Wrong, Miss Curly, Mr Chatty, Miss Goody, Mr Slow, Miss Talky-Talky, Mr Complain, Miss Shy, Mr Generous, Miss Mouth (someone who talks all the time or tells secrets), Mr What (someone who never knows what the group is talking about), Miss Why (someone who always asks questions), Mr Busy, Miss Skinny, Mr Late.

Variations

Make it difficult

The children stick their photos on the 'Our nicknames' poster. They write their nickname next to each photo, and the reasons for their nickname, for example:

I'm Mr Quiet because I never talk.
I'm Miss Mouth because I always tell secrets.

Links

You may link this activity with: **Paper-bag faces (31)**.

Teacher's diary

Did the children enjoy the nicknames that were given to them? Did they accept them? Can they remember each other's nickname easily? Did they feel they learned many new words? Do you think this can help them use the new words in different contexts?

12 Families

Topic	Family
Activity type	Socialising
Language	Words related to the topic; words related to animals
Time	40–50 minutes
Classroom setting	Any
Materials	A large sheet of paper, a set of pictures of families (e.g. a bear family, a duck family, a dog family, a fish family), crayons
Age	6–12
Level	Elementary
Purpose	Becoming familiar with the words related to the 'family'

In class

1. Hang the sheet of paper on the wall. List your name and the names of all the children on the left side of it. Draw a rectangular box next to each name. Draw the members of your family in the box next to your name. Say:

   This is my mother, this is my father, this is my husband, these are my two children and this is me. (Obviously, change it according to your family situation.)

   Invite the children — one after the other — to make drawings of all the members of their families. Each child does a drawing and tells the relationship following your model. Ask them questions like:

   Is this your brother? Brother? Yes, your brother. Say 'This is my (touch your chest) brother.'

NAME	FAMILY	HOW MANY
ANNA		4

2. Write on the top right side of the poster

> How many?

Make the children count the members of each family and write the number next to each drawing under the heading 'How many?' Say:

> In my family there are six people. My mother, my father, my husband, my two children and me.

Point at each person in the drawing while you mention them. The children do the same following your example.

Variations

Expand

(1)   Show the pictures of the families. Say:

> This is a bear family. Can you see Mother Bear here, and Father Bear and this is Baby Bear.

Do the same with the other pictures.

(2)   Divide the children into groups of three to six members. Be a member of one group yourself. Say:

> Now we play families. Let's be a bear family.

The children decide within each group who is going to be Mother Bear, Father Bear, etc. They take their own role and pretend to behave like the members of the bear family (e.g. the big one in the group will be Father Bear and will behave protectively, Mother Bear will walk arm in arm with him and Baby Bear will jump playfully around them trying to 'climb' on their bodies). When all the children have had the chance to behave like a bear, change family. Say:

Now we are a duck family.

The children pretend to be a duck family. Encourage them also to produce the appropriate animal sounds. Remember also to say:

Now let's be a human family.

Make it difficult

When playing families encourage the children to use some language routines that may be pronounced with the accent of the family the children are pretending to be.

Links

You may link this activity with: **Races (13)**; **First day at school (22)**; **Our little people (25)**; **Let's pretend we are animals (28)**.

Teacher's diary

How did the children do in this activity? What other language-learning activities can you build up around the topic 'Families'?

---

13 Races

Topic	Races, nationalities
Activity type	Socialising
Language	Words related to the topic
Time	40–50 minutes
Classroom setting	Any
Materials	A map of the world, pictures of children from different countries, crayons, blue-tack, a make-up set, dressing-up clothes
Age	8–11
Level	Elementary
Purpose	Becoming aware of different races and cultures; becoming familiar with words related to 'nationalities'

Preparation

Bring pictures of children from different countries of the world (e.g. native Americans, Afro-Americans, Indians, Asians, Africans, Brazilians).

In class

1. **(In L1)** Show the pictures and invite the children to look at the various physical features that they can discover. Ask them if they can imagine the nationality of the children in the pictures.

2. Stick the map of the world on the wall. Show the countries that the children in the pictures belong to. Ask your students to stick the pictures on the appropriate country. Give them some general information about these different countries and cultures.

43

3. **(In L2)**   Focus on nationalities. Say:

    This girl is Chinese, this boy is African.

    while pointing at the pictures. The children repeat the nationalities.

4. Focus on physical features. Tell the children to choose one race — among the
    ones mentioned before — and invite them to 'make up' as if they belonged to
    that race; for example:

    Indian girls will have a coloured round mark between their eyes.
    Native Americans will put feathers around their heads.
    Japanese will adjust the shape of their eyes.
    Afro-Americans will colour their skin dark.

    When the children have completed their make-up, ask: 'Who is Japanese?', 'Who
    is Afro-American?', etc.
    Let them walk around the classroom and tell each other: 'I'm Indian. What's
    your nationality?'

5. Group them according to 'races'. Then ask: 'How many Asians are there?', 'How
    many Afro-Americans are there?', etc.

Variations

Make it easier

If you have a group of younger children play 'Ring-a-ring-a-rosy' first with 'single-
race' groups, then with 'mixed-race' groups.

Links

You may link this activity with: **Families (12)**.

Teacher's diary

Did the children find this activity interesting? How much did they learn
about other races? Did they enjoy dressing-up like somebody from
another country? What other language-learning activities can you build
up around the topic 'Races'? Would you consider any link with
geography themes? Or with the communicative function 'describing
people'?

14 Show and tell

Topic	Any chosen by the child
Activity type	Socialising
Language	Simple expressions related to the communicative function 'describing things'
Background knowledge	Basic knowledge of 'how to describe things'
Time	30—40 minutes
Classroom setting	Any
Materials	Objects children bring from home
Age	7 and above
Level	From elementary to advanced, depending on the expected complexity of children's descriptions
Purpose	Encouraging children to talk about their favourite objects

Preparation

Together with the children decide on a day (say Thursday) when each week you will perform 'Show and tell'. Tell the children that, on 'Show-and-tell day', they can bring an object (a toy, a drawing, a book, some photos) from home to show to the class.

Review the basic language expressions related to the communicative functions of 'describing something', 'talking about something' and 'expressing opinions about something'; for example:

This is a . . .
I use this for . . .
I like it a lot.

I love it.
This is my favourite . . .
This reminds me of . . .
etc.

In class

On 'Show-and-tell day' write the expressions mentioned above on the blackboard as a guideline for the children. In turn, they show their objects to the class and describe them using as much L2 as they can; for example:

This is my toy lorry. It's my favourite toy. I love it. I play with it after school.

Do not expect the children to be extremely accurate. Accept even one word or one sentence. Provide new words if the children need them for the description.

Variations

Make it difficult

Let a group of children 'show and tell' about their objects. Ask the other children to make a report on what their peers have said.

Links

You may link this activity with: **Your 'closest' pen-friend (86)**.

Teacher's diary

How well did the activity go? Did the children enjoy bringing objects from home? Did they need lots of help from you before and while talking about their objects? Did you have to tell them many new words? Did they find it useful?

---

15 Who's got the ring?

Activity type Socialising

Language 'Who's got . . .'; '_____ has got the _____'; 'Yes, I've got it'; 'No, I haven't got it'

Background knowledge The children should have been introduced to the verb 'to have'

Time 40—45 minutes

Classroom setting Children sitting in a circle

Materials A ring

Age 7—13

Level Elementary

Purpose Practising how to express possession

Preparation

Remind the children of the expressions that they need to use when talking about possession. If the children have been introduced to L2 written skills, write a short outline on the blackboard to help them remember the expressions they are going to use.

In class

Arrange the children in a circle. Give the ring to a child. She holds it between her hands, which have to be put in a palm-to-palm position as in a prayer. The child goes around the circle while the classmates keep their hands in the same position. One after the other, the child puts her hands inside her peers' hands. Before the round is completed she hides the ring in another child's hands.

Say:

Who's got the ring?

The children make their guesses by saying:

Mario has got it.

If Mario has the ring he says:

Yes, I've got it.

If he does not have the ring, he says:

No, I haven't got it

and shows this by opening his hands. The guessing continues until the children discover who has got the ring. The child who guessed correctly has the right to make the new round.

Variations

If nobody has got a ring in the classroom, choose any other small object.

Links

You may link this activity with: **The classroom band (53)**; **Inventory (59)**.

Teacher's diary

How did the children like this game? Did they all get involved easily? Was it difficult for them to produce the expressions of possession at the beginning of the game? Did they improve during the game? If yes, why? Was it because of the repetitive use of them? Did they look self-confident in using the expressions at the end of the game?

SECTION II

GAMES CHILDREN LIKE TO PLAY

16 Nonsense language

Topic	Foreign languages and nonsense language
Activity type	Language play
Time	15–20 minutes
Classroom setting	Any
Materials	An audio-cassette with short extracts of L2 conversations; a tape-recorder
Age	6 and above
Level	Beginner
Purpose	Helping children become aware of the concept of 'foreign language'; helping them become familiar with 'strange' sounds; encouraging children to play with sounds

Preparation

Prepare a cassette with short extracts of conversations in the L2 that the children are going to learn.

In class

1. Ask the children what 'foreign language' means to them. Elicit their answers and give your explanation. Tell them to name some 'foreign languages'. Ask if they have ever heard these languages spoken. How did they sound to them? Or, if they have never heard a foreign language spoken, how do they think it may sound?

    Let them think for a little while. Some of them may start a 'nonsense' language with 'nonsense' sounds made up by themselves. If this happens, encourage them to use these sounds for a short while. Encourage the other children who may still be silent to do the same.

2. Get the tape-recorder. Let the children listen to the extracts of conversations in the foreign language that they are going to learn. Stop the tape. How did the language sound to them? Did they like the sounds? Did the language sound gentle to them? Did it sound rough?

Variations

Make it difficult

Tape extracts of conversations in several languages on the cassette. Let the children listen to the extracts. How did the languages sound to them? Did they recognise any? Which ones would they like to learn? Focus on the one they are going to learn. Do they like it? How does it sound to them?, etc. (Continue as in 2.)

Links

You may link this activity with: **The funny answer (17)**; **Sounds (18)**.

Teacher's diary

Did the children find this activity interesting? Or funny? How did they react to your encouragement to produce 'nonsense' sounds? Did they produce any 'nonsense' sounds or were they too shy? How did they react to the tape extracts?

---

17 The funny answer

Topic	Unfamiliar language
Activity type	Language play
Language	Language related to the topic
Time	10–15 minutes
Classroom setting	Any
Materials	A set of L2 expressions
Age	6 and above
Level	Beginner
Purpose	Encouraging children to play with unfamiliar language; helping children become familiar with 'strange' expressions

Preparation

Prepare a set of expressions unknown to the children.

In class

1. **(In L1)** Tell the children you are going to talk to them in the L2. You will ask them questions, report and explain things to them. They will probably not understand but they are free to answer as follows:

   Keeping silent.
   Smiling.
   Laughing.
   With a funny answer in their L1.
   With a funny answer using a nonsense language.
   Any other way they want to.

(In L2)   Talk to them in a lively way. Make gestures while you talk. Talk to them one by one to give each of them the chance to provide the 'funny answer'. Make this 'unusual conversation' last for a few minutes until the children pay attention to what you say and enjoy each other's answers. Stop the conversation as soon as enjoyment fades away.

2.   **(In L1)**   When the conversation is over, ask them if they have understood anything you said to them and what they think it was. Can they recall any words or expressions? Can they repeat them now? Appreciate any effort that they make to guess the meaning of your talking even though it may be wrong. If nobody is aware of anything you said, tell the general meaning of your conversation.

Variations

Make it difficult and expand

Write those few words or expressions that the children can recall. Check their comprehension of meaning. Ask them to read the expressions aloud.

Links

You may link this activity with: **Nonsense language (16)**; **Sounds (18)**.

Teacher's diary

How did the activity work? Did the children find the activity funny? How did they react to what you were telling them? Were they able to recall any new expressions?

---

18 Sounds

Topic	L2 sounds
Activity type	Language play
Time	20–25 minutes
Classroom setting	Children sitting in a circle
Materials	A set of L2 sounds; a set of flashcards with words; a set of flashcards with pictures; blu-tack
Age	6 and above
Level	Beginner
Purpose	Playing with sounds; getting familiar with new sounds; recognising words from sounds

Preparation

Make a selection of L2 sounds that you think the children may find difficult to produce; for example:

[dʒ], [θ], [tʃ], [dr], [tr], [h]

Select a set of words that have these sounds as beginning sounds; for example:

jet, thumb, choo-choo train, church, dress, train, hamburger.

Choose words that may be familiar — e.g. L2 words used in their L1.

Prepare a set of flashcards and write the words on them. Prepare another set of flashcards and make drawings that represent the words on them.

In class

1. Arrange the children in a circle sitting on chairs or on the floor. Sit together with them as a member of the circle. Create an atmosphere of complete silence. Turn

towards the child sitting next to you and say the first sound (e.g. [dʒ]). The child turns towards her peer sitting beside her and repeats the sound. This goes on until the round has been completed and the 'passing' sound has reached you again.

Say a new sound and have another round in the way you have done before. Go on like this until your list is completed. Every three or four sounds introduce one of the selected 'words' that begins with one of the 'sounds' you are playing with.

2. When the game is over, have some feedback from the children. Can they recall the sounds? Have they understood that you have also introduced words? Have they recognised the words from the sounds? Can they recall the words?

Variations

Make it difficult and expand

1. When the children repeat the sounds say the words that match with them and show the pictures to provide the meaning. Make them repeat these new words.

2. Stick the pictures on the wall. Show the flashcards with the words written on them. Read the words and ask the children to repeat them after you.

3. Give the flashcards to the children. Ask them to match the words with the pictures by sticking the flashcards under the appropriate pictures.

4. Let them read the words aloud.

Links

You may link this activity with: **Nonsense language (16)**; **The funny answer (17)**; **The onomatopoeic game (19)**; **The dictionary poster (42)**.

Teacher's diary

Did the children enjoy playing with sounds? Did they find it funny? Were they able to recognise the words from the sounds? Do you think that they feel more familiar with new difficult sounds now?

---

19   The onomatopoeic game

Topic	L2 onomatopoeic sounds
Activity type	Language play
Language	Onomatopoeic words
Time	30—40 minutes
Classroom setting	Any
Materials	A list of L2 onomatopoeic sounds; a set of cut-outs from cartoons showing onomatopoeic sounds; or cut-out objects/ activities from magazines; a large sheet of paper
Age	8 and above
Level	Elementary—intermediate
Purpose	Getting to know the concept of 'onomatopoeia'; getting familiar with onomatopoeic words

Preparation

Prepare a list of onomatopoeic sounds that you think may be enjoyable for the children. Find these sounds in cartoons or pictures that illustrate the sounds in magazines. Cut them out ready to be shown to the children.

In class

1. Teach the concept of 'onomatopoeia'. Ask the children if they already know some onomatopoeic sounds. Let them say and play with these sounds by miming the actions. Tell the children that onomatopoeic words sometimes differ from one language to another. Give some examples like the ones I am suggesting here:

	ENGLISH	ITALIAN	SPANISH	FRENCH
(someone at the door)	knock-knock	toc toc	tan tan	toc toc
(dog)	woof-woof	bau bau	guau guau	ouah ouah
(clock)	tick tock	tic tac	tic tac	tic tac
(telephone)	ring ring	drin drin	ring ring	drring drring
(food)	crunch crunch	gnam gnam	chump chump	croc croc
(bee)	buzz	zzz	zzz zzz	bzzz bzzz
(snake)	hiss	hiss	ss ssh	ss ss
(mouse)	squeak squeak	squeak	iii iii	iii iii

2. Show the cut-outs from cartoons and/or the pictures. Focus on the onomatopoeic sounds represented on them.

3. Start the game. Divide the children into two groups. One group mime a sound, the other guess the onomatopoeic word related to it. Exchange roles between the two groups.

4. Go to the blackboard. Ask the children to dictate the onomatopoeic words they know by now. Write them. Let the children read them aloud.

5. Get the sheet of paper. Write 'Our onomatopoeic poster' at the top of it. Get the children to stick the cut-outs on it. They can add their own drawings if they wish. They choose the appropriate onomatopoeic words among those written on the blackboard and write them next to (or under) each picture in large coloured letters.

Variations

Make it difficult

If the children in your class are ready for written activities, help them prepare a matching list of onomatopoeic words in L1 and L2. The aim is to check which words are the same, which are different, which have been 'borrowed' from the L2.

Links

You may link this activity with: **Sounds (18)**.

Teacher's diary

How well did the activity go? Were the children interested in onomatopoeic sounds? Had they come across these sounds before? In what contexts? Cartoons? Children's magazines? Which step of this activity has best contributed to help the children remember the meaning of the sounds that you have presented?

20   I say, you repeat

Activity type	Language play
Language	Based on your selection of sentences
Background knowledge	The children need to know some of the expressions that you have selected
Time	20–30 minutes
Classroom setting	Any
Materials	A set of flashcards. Each card will have one of the expressions that you have selected written on it
Age	8 and above
Level	Elementary–intermediate, depending on the complexity of the expressions
Purpose	Showing comprehension through repetition

Preparation

Prepare a set of L2 expressions that the children are already familiar with. Add a few new expressions.

In class

1. **(In L1)** Explain to the children the following rules:

   - If you recognise the sentence and understand the meaning repeat it aloud.

   - If you do not recognise the sentence but the sounds of the words seem familiar to you whisper the sentence.

   - If you do not recognise the sentence, nor are the sounds familiar to you, keep silent.

(In L2)   Read one sentence (without showing the flashcard). Look around and encourage the children's reactions: some may repeat, some may whisper, some may keep silent. Read another sentence, check the reactions and so on until you complete your list of sentences. There will be some confusion in the classroom but this is part of the game.

2.   When your list has been completed, write the following scheme on the blackboard:

> 1. Know   2. Maybe   3. Don't know

Ask the children to think back to the expressions you have said so far. Then follow these steps:

> Do they remember any? Can they say them? Do they know the meaning? Do they know when they have to use them?

Yes? Show the flashcard related to the expressions. Let the children read the expressions and stick the cards under the 'know' column.

> Can they remember any of the sentences that they whispered? Can they repeat any?

Yes? Show the flashcards to them and explain the meaning. Let them read the expressions and stick the card under the 'maybe' column.

Variations

Make it difficult

If the children are not able to repeat or do not remember any of the new expressions, introduce them, explain their use and put them under the 'don't know' column. Do it only if you think that the extra language will not crowd the children's minds too much.

Links

You may link this activity with: **Rush the sentence (4)**.

Teacher's diary

How many sentences did the children recognise? Did they look self-confident when they were repeating them? Could they remember any of the new expressions?

---

21 L2 'borrowing' game

Topic	L2 borrowings
Activity type	Learning and recognising words
Language	Words related to the topic/L2 borrowings
Background knowledge	The children should know some basic words related to the topic
Time	30–40 minutes
Classroom setting	Any
Materials	A set of L2 words that are used in the children's first language; a large sheet of paper
Age	7 and above
Level	Beginner–elementary
Purpose	Becoming aware of 'foreign' words used in the mother tongue; adjusting inappropriate pronunciation; becoming aware of the use of L2 borrowings in the L1

Preparation

Make a list of well-known L2 words that are used in the children's first language.

In class

1. Write this set of L2 words on the blackboard. Read the words to the children in the way they are usually pronounced in the children's first language. Tell the children that, although these words sound familiar to them, they are not L1 words but have been 'borrowed' from the L2.

2. Read the words again but this time do it with the appropriate pronunciation. The children repeat after you, first. Then, read the words and explain the meaning.

3. Ask the children to make up expressions in their L1 in which they use the words that you have listed on the blackboard. Write their expressions on a large sheet of paper. Highlight the L2 words with a marker. Stick the poster on the wall to remind the children of the L2 'borrowings'.

Variations

Make it difficult

Ask the children to make up expressions in their L1 in which they use L2 words that they know from their previous lessons — this time the words do not have to be real L2 borrowings. The children's task is to show their ability to use the L2 words in an appropriate L1 context, for example (Italian):

> A me piace l'icecream
> Voglio andare alla beach
> Io ho a bicycle

Put this 'follow-up' into practice when the children have only competence at the word level and have not mastered competence at the sentence level yet. In fact, it would be 'unnatural' to encourage the production of such sentences when the children can already produce full L2 sentences.

Links

You may link this activity with: **The dictionary poster (42)**; **Search for the English word (57)**.

Teacher's diary

How did the children perform during this activity? Did they already know any borrowings used in their mother tongue? Has this activity helped them become aware of their meaning and use?

22 First day at school

Topic	School time
Activity type	Sociodramatic play
Language	Communicative function of 'persuading'
Time	40–50 minutes
Classroom setting	In the playground or at the gym, if available; in the classroom, but desks should be back to the walls to create enough space for the children to move around
Age	7–11
Level	Elementary–intermediate
Purpose	Encouraging children to think of their first school day; learning how to persuade

In class

1. **(In L1)** Tell the children to think about their first day at school. Encourage them to think and talk about it. What did they say? Who took them there: mothers, fathers, grandparents, nannies? What did mothers, fathers or nannies say when they had to leave? What did the teachers say? Note down these expressions. Tell them that, like them, L2 children do not always like to go to school the very first time.

2. **(In L2)** Select some simple expressions that the children have mentioned. Say the expressions in the L2. Let them repeat. Write on the blackboard:

   Me   Mother/Father/Nanny   Teacher

   Write the expressions that they have learned under the appropriate columns (e.g. the children's expressions under 'Me', the mothers' expressions under 'Mother', etc.). Help them read the expressions.

3. Divide the children into three groups. One group plays the role of 'children', another plays the role of 'mothers or fathers', and the third group plays the role of 'teachers'. The three groups should know what expressions to use by now.

    The play starts, and it should be a confusion of crying children who run away from their mothers, angry mothers pushing them, smiling teachers who try to encourage the children to go to school. There should be, therefore, a screaming of:

    > NO! NO! NO! GO HOME! GO HOME! Let's go home.
    > COME! COME! School is nice!
    > TOMORROW, TOMORROW.
    > But TODAY is the first day.
    > Come, we play here

    and a few others.

    There will be lots of screaming but also lots of fun for the children.

Variations

Make it difficult

Expand the expressions with faster or more advanced learners. Help them produce expressions like: 'I don't want to go!', 'I want to go back home!', 'Let's come back tomorrow!', 'I don't like to go!', 'I want to go with grandma!'

Links

You may link this activity with: **Families (12)**; **Play shop (23)**; **Going to the doctor (24)**.

Teacher's diary

Which step of the activity did the children enjoy best? Did they like talking about their first day at school? Did they enjoy their roles during the dramatisation? Was it easy for them to remember the expressions they had to say during the performance?

---

23 Play shop

Topic	Shopping
Activity type	Sociodramatic play
Language	'How much is it?'; 'It's [amount of money]'
Background knowledge	The children should know about department stores and shopping habits in the L2 countries; numbers; expressions related to money
Time	50–60 minutes
Classroom setting	Desks displayed as department-store stands, children around the classroom
Materials	A large box; any merchandise from home; cards for labels
Age	8 and above
Level	Elementary and intermediate
Purpose	Getting familiar with shopping habits, expressions related to money, the communicative function of 'asking for something'

Preparation

Bring in 'goods' from home that may be found in a supermarket; e.g. soap, toothpaste, fruit, biscuits, toys, clothes.

Collect these goods for a few days and keep them in a large box. Ask the children to add any other goods to your collection that they have available.

Introduce the L2 words for these objects and prepare labels for them.

In class

When the box is full of little things, the classroom can be turned into a 'department store'.

Follow these steps with the help of the children:

- Organise the stands with all the goods on them.
- Match the labels with the objects and put the labels near the objects.
- Price the merchandise and make paper money.
- Ask the children to read the prices aloud.
- Introduce 'How much is the ...?', 'Can I see it?', 'I'll buy it.'
- Write these new expressions on the blackboard.
- Ask for extra simple expressions that can be used in department stores. Elicit them from the children or suggest them.
- Write these expressions on the blackboard as a guide for the game.
- Decide who plays the role of shop assistants and who plays the role of customers.

Shopping begins.

Children go from one stand to another buying goods. They produce expressions like 'Good morning! Can I see ...?', 'How much is this ...?', 'It's ...', 'This is nice', 'Look', 'This?', 'The red one.'

Let the children take turns in their roles. Do not worry if the expressions are not accurate during the role play. What matters, at this point, is that they use as much language as they can.

Variations

Expand

The children check who bought what and who bought more. They make a list of the goods that each child bought.

Links

You may link this activity with: **First day at school (22)**; **Going to the doctor (24)**.

Teacher's diary

Was it easy to organise the shop? Could the children remember the shopping expressions? How did they perform? Which step of the activity did they like best? How would you improve the activity if you had classroom organisational problems?

24 Going to the doctor

Topic	Going to the doctor
Activity type	Sociodramatic play
Language	Lexical items and expressions related to the topic
Background knowledge	The children should have some basic 'role-play' experience and basic oral and reading skills
Time	Two periods of 45 minutes
Classroom setting	The classroom will be arranged into a doctor's waiting room or a doctor's office
Materials	A set* of toy objects that can be used by a doctor or a nurse, e.g. spectacles, band-aid, a thermometer, sweets, etc.; a dialogue model to use as a guide
Age	8—11
Level	Intermediate and advanced
Purpose	Talking about personal experiences; learning about medical customs in the L2 countries; using appropriate language for specific social settings

Preparation

Prepare a dialogue which you may use as a guide to build up the sketches with the children.

*This can be a set of 'real' toys or it may well be a set of toys created by the children; e.g. strips of adhesive-tape can become plasters, a pen can become the thermometer, etc.

In class

1. **(In L1)**   Ask the children if they have ever been to the doctor's. Ask them the following:

    *   What they saw.
    *   What they heard said.
    *   What they did.
    *   What they were asked to do.
    *   What feelings they had.

    Show interest in what they say. Note down their comments on the left side of the blackboard.

2. Tell them that at the doctor's children usually do the following:

    Wait in a waiting room where they at times find toys to play with.
    Meet a nurse first.
    The nurse brings the child and the parents into a room, asks the child her
      name and age.
    The nurse takes the child and the parents into the doctor's room.
    The doctor examines the child.
    The child gets a treat at the end of the visit.

3. **(In L2)**   Draw the following on the blackboard:

    a doctor, a nurse, a waiting room, a doctor's room, other doctor's objects.

    Teach the appropriate words, orally first. Then write the words under each drawing and ask the children to read them. Tell them:

    Now we are going to play doctors.

    With their help, arrange the classroom into a waiting room and a doctor's office. Prepare labels for these two rooms.

4. Go back to the blackboard. Check what you have noted down on its left side. Provide English expressions and write them down on the right side. Use these expressions as a databank to build up a dialogue with the help of the children. If necessary, use some ideas from the dialogue that you have previously prepared. At the same time, try to elicit as many ideas and language suggestions from the children. Ask them guide questions (use L1) like the following:

    What would you say when you meet the nurse?
    What would you answer at this point?
    What would you say to the doctor?
    What would the doctor tell the child now?

    Write the dialogue on the blackboard or use an overhead projector, if available.

5. Give each child a role chosen from the following:

    the nurse, the doctor, another doctor, a secretary, the child, the mother, the
    father, other children in the waiting room

    or any other roles you can think of. Add as many as you can in order to involve
    every child in the game.

6. Give them some time to rehearse their part.

7. The performance starts. Enjoy it. Note down comments, mistakes, suggestions.
    Report these to the children and give feedback to them when the performance
    is over.

Variations

Optional follow-up

Prepare a set of sheets with the dialogue 'The doctor' written on them. Leave
some words or expressions blank. Give a sheet to each child. They complete the
dialogue by filling in the blanks.

Links

You may link this activity with: **First day at school (22)**; **Play shop (23)**.

Teacher's diary

How did the activity work? Were the roles easy or difficult for the
children? How did they perform? Did they make mistakes while
performing? How did you correct them?

---

25   Our little people

Topic	People
Activity type	Playing fantasy games
Language	Giving personal information about other people
Background knowledge	The children should be able to give personal information about other people
Time	30−40 minutes
Classroom setting	Children sitting around Lego-people pieces
Materials	Lego people or any other toys chosen by the children (e.g. coloured rods)
Age	7 and above
Level	Elementary−intermediate
Purpose	Practising the communicative function of 'giving personal information about a third person'

Preparation

Ask the children to bring in any toys that make them think of 'people'; for example, people that belong to Lego sets etc., coloured rods, wooden blocks that may become people with a little imagination. Provide these materials if the children do not have enough.

In class

Let the children sit in a circle. Collect the pieces and lay them on a chair or on the floor in the centre of the circle. Encourage the children to make up an identity for each 'man' or 'woman' and talk about them. Let them think for a little while, then ask:

What's his/her name?
How old is s/he?
Does s/he go to school? Does s/he like school?
What are his/her hobbies?
Does s/he have a brother or a sister?
(Add any other questions appropriate to your class.)

Elicit answers from the children and try to get as much information as they can provide.

If some children have been silent during the activity, ask them to report the information provided by the others; for example:

> (pointing to the man)   This is Johnny. He is nine years old. He goes to school. He likes school. He likes football and skateboards. He has one brother and two sisters.

Variations

Make it difficult

Ask the children to select one 'man' or 'woman' and write a short paragraph about them. The children read each other's paragraphs.

Links

You may link this activity with: **Families (12)**.

Teacher's diary

Were the children able to make up identities for the 'people'? Were all the children involved?

26 The micro-cities

Topic	Cities
Activity type	Playing realistic games
Language	Words related to city places; prepositions of place
Time	40–50 minutes
Classroom setting	Children around micro-cities
Materials	Micro-toys, coloured rods, wooden blocks, a set of small self-adhesive cards
Age	7 and above
Level	Elementary–intermediate
Purpose	Introducing and practising names of places; saying where places are

Preparation

Ask those children who have sets of micro-toys at home to bring them to school. Bring in coloured rods yourself and wooden blocks or anything that could be used to build up a city.

In class

1. Display the materials on the floor or on a table. The children sit down around them. Ask the children to adapt the materials in such a way as to build up a 'micro-city' by using their imagination.

   When the city is ready, ask the children the names of the places that can be found in it; for example:

   a garage, an airport, a bar, a petrol station, a car wash, a police station

Provide the names in English if they do not know them. Let them repeat the names after you.

Write the names of places on the cards and stick the cards in the appropriate place.

2. Ask 'Where is the garage?' etc. They answer by pointing at the places.

3. Introduce 'Here', 'Over there.' Go on asking: 'Where is the . . .?' The children — this time — point to the objects and produce the new expressions 'Here', 'Over there.'

4. Introduce some prepositions of place by saying sentences such as:

   The garage is next to the petrol station.

   Let them repeat the prepositions after you when you say the sentences. Stress your voice when you say 'next to', 'near', 'opposite'.

   Go on asking 'Where is the . . .?' (or ask a child to do it for you). The children try now to produce the full sentences; for example:

   The garage is opposite the airport.

Round-up

5. Go to the blackboard. Ask the children to say the names of the places in the city. Elicit the names and write them at random on the blackboard. Help the children read the names.

6. Elicit the prepositions. Write them on the blackboard. Highlight the prepositions by surrounding each of them by a small square (or use coloured chalk). Ask the children to make up sentences with the words written on the blackboard.

Follow-up

Help them to make drawings of micro-cities. They complete the drawings by writing the appropriate names of places.

Variations

Expand

Introduce street directions like the following: 'Go straight on', 'Turn', 'Turn left', 'Turn right', 'Stop there', 'Cross'. Play a 'follow-me' game with street directions. One child says 'I am near the garage. Follow me! I go straight, I turn right. I cross . . . and I stop. Where am I?'

Links

You may link this activity with: **Follow the leader (6)**; **Closer — closer! (30)**; **What's missing? (32)**; **Blind steps (61)**.

27 Let's pretend we are weather forecasters

Topic	Weather
Activity type	Playing 'let's pretend'
Language	'It's rainy', 'it's sunny', 'it's windy'. 'Take the . . .', 'Put . . . on'
Background knowledge	Simple present of the verb 'to be'; the children should be able to use expressions related to weather features (e.g. 'it's rainy', 'it's sunny', etc.)
Time	40−45 minutes
Classroom setting	Children standing in the centre of the classroom or any other large space
Materials	Drawings related to weather features, some umbrellas, scarves, woollen hats, straw hats, paper fans
Age	6 and above
Level	Elementary
Purpose	Practising 'weather' expressions

Preparation

Introduce expressions about weather features (cold, hot, rainy, cloudy, etc.) with the aid of pictures.* When the children start being familiar with the expressions, ask them to make their own drawings following the models you have previously shown.

In class

1. Divide the class into two groups of 'weather forecasters'. One group (G1) keeps the drawings of 'bad weather', the other (G2) keeps the drawings of 'good weather'.

*This should have been done in a previous lesson.

A third, smaller group (G3) pretends to be 'children in the playground'. This third group will use objects, such as umbrellas, scarves, woollen hats, straw hats, paper fans, boots, etc.

2. The G3 children start playing in the playground. G1 and G2, in turn, 'make' the weather by holding up a drawing at a time. G3 check the weather and shout at each other the appropriate expression; for example:

    rainy drawing → 'It's raining, it's raining! Get your umbrella.' (They open their umbrellas.)
    cloudy drawing → 'It's not raining. Close your umbrella.'
    snowy drawing → 'It's snowing. Get your boots.'/'Put your boots on.'
    sunny drawing → 'It's sunny, it's sunny! Get your straw hat.' (They put the straw hats on.)
    windy drawing → 'It's windy, it's windy! Get your scarf.' (They put scarves on.) etc.

    Make sure that the game is performed quickly. Allow the children to switch from one group to another.

Variations

Expand

At the end of the game the children hang their drawings on the wall. Write the weather expressions on the blackboard. Help the children read the expressions. Ask them to copy the expressions on their drawings.

Make it difficult

Bring in newspaper cut-outs of 'weather forecasts'. Help the children to read the symbols.

Links

You may link this activity with: **Date, weather, time, the register (35)**; **Make your own calendar (36)**; **Hopscotch (74)**.

Teacher's diary

How did the activity go? Was it difficult to organise? Did all the children have the chance to be in the three groups? Did they like performing 'in the playground'? Did they make any spontaneous changes to their performance? What other language-learning activities could you prepare around the topic 'Weather'?

28 Let's pretend we are animals

Topic   Animals

Activity type   Playing 'let's pretend'

Language   Words related to the topic

Background   The children should know the meaning of 'let's pretend'
knowledge

Time   20−30 minutes

Classroom   Children standing around the classroom
setting

Materials   Books that show pictures of animals, pictures of animals
                       cut out of magazines, blu-tack

Age   6 and above

Level   Elementary

Purpose   Learning and recognising vocabulary related to animals and
                       their environment

Preparation

Prepare a set of pictures of animals. Include also pictures of baby animals.

In class

1. Show the pictures of the animals to the children. Introduce (or review) their names.
    Introduce also words such as 'baby animals', 'cubs', 'puppies', 'kittens',
    'ducklings'.

2. Write on the blackboard in large letters:

    Forest, Sea, Farm, Desert

Make simple drawings next to each name to explain the meaning of these words.

Ask the children which environment the animals in the pictures belong to. Invite them to stick the pictures under (or around) the appropriate 'environment' word.

3.   Arrange the children in a circle in the centre of the classroom. Tell them:

Let's pretend we are animals in the forest.

Say:

Horse.

Start galloping and invite the children to do the same. Stop and say:

Snake.

Bend your body and crawl close to the ground. The children do it, too. Say:

Bear.

Expect the children to move around like bears. Change environment. Say:

Let's pretend we are animals on the farm.

Say:

Dog.

Wait for the children to bark. Continue until you have completed the set of animals in the pictures.

When the children become familiar with the names of the animals, ask one of them to take your role and call the names of the animals for the group.

Variations

Make it difficult

At later stages play the same game but make it more difficult by introducing the words for the different kinds of movements that the animals do, for example:

A horse gallops.
A snake wriggles on the ground.
A dog barks and runs.
A chimpanzee plays in the tree.
A bird flies.
A kangaroo jumps.
A lion roars.
A fish swims in the water.
(Add any other you want.)

Expect the children to do the animal actions that you mention.

Links

You may link this activity with: **Families (12)**; **Hopscotch (34)**; **Jigsaw story (71)**.

Teacher's diary

Did the children enjoy this activity? Did they learn a large number of new words? Can they remember them easily?

---

29   Chase and catch

Topic	Run, chase and support
Activity type	Supporting classmates
Language	'Can/can't', 'catch'
Background knowledge	'Him'/'her'
Time	30 minutes
Classroom setting	Large space needed, possibly outside
Age	6–11
Level	Beginner–elementary
Purpose	Learning how to give support

Preparation

1. Explain (or remind) the meaning of 'can/can't'. Remind the children of the difference between 'him' and 'her'.

2. Tell them about the roles that supporters and 'cheer leaders' have during sports games. Bring pictures, if you have any, to show how cheer leaders dress, what jumps and body movements they make.

3. Tell them that many children often play 'run and chase'. They run away from a chaser while shouting the tuned phrase:

   You can't catch me, you can't catch me.

In class

Choose two runners: a chaser and a chased. Divide the class into two opposing groups.

One group plays in favour of the chaser, the other group plays in favour of the chased.

The runners start the game. They run around until the chaser catches the other. In the meanwhile, the two groups support the runners by shouting:

You can't catch him/her, you can't catch him/her

in support of the chased and

You can catch him/her, you can catch him/her

in support of the chaser.

Let the children be free to shout and move as they like. Give all the children the chance to be runners at least once.

After a while, introduce extra 'supporting' expressions such as:

Come on! You can do it. Run! Run away! Go! Go faster! Run faster!

Variations

Have three runners: a chaser and two chased. The other children will shout: 'You can't catch them!' or 'You can catch them!'

Links

You may link this activity with: **The crazy train (7)**.

Teacher's diary

Did the children get involved in the activity easily? Did they support each other as you expected? Was it genuine support given in the second/foreign language?

30 Closer — closer!

Activity type	Learning and recognising words
Language	'Close', 'closer', 'far', 'farther', 'here', 'there'
Time	20—30 minutes
Classroom setting	Any
Materials	Any object
Age	7 and above
Level	Beginner—elementary
Purpose	Getting familiar with 'distance' words

Preparation

Teach the children 'distance words' like 'close', 'closer', 'far', 'farther', 'here', 'there'. Explain the difference between 'close, far' and 'closer, farther'. Introduce the idea of 'cold', 'warmer', 'hot', 'very hot' to estimate proximity to the object. When you consider that they are getting familiar with these words start the game.

In class

Choose a small object that you find in the classroom (e.g. a small ball, a rubber, a pencil, a sticker, etc.). Select a 'child' who leaves the room. The children hide the object. Call the 'child' back into the classroom and tell her to search for the object.

While the child walks around the room the other children guide her by saying the 'distance words' or the 'cold words'. If the child gets close to the object, the children say 'close/closer' or 'warm/warmer'. If she moves away from the object, the children say 'far/farther' or 'cold/colder'. When the child gets very close to the object, the children say 'there/very hot' and help their classmate find it.

Give other children the chance to be the 'searching child', if they wish to.

Variations

Make it difficult

Introduce other words and phrases that the children might use while their peers are searching: 'to the right', 'to the left', 'Be careful on the right', 'Search in front of you', etc.

In some countries 'fire' and 'water' are used instead of 'hot' and 'cold'.

Links

You may link this activity with: **The micro-cities (26)**.

Teacher's diary

Did the children enjoy searching for the hidden object? Was it easy for them to get familiar with 'distance' words? Did they prefer the hot/cold words?

31 Paper-bag faces

Topic	Feelings
Activity type	Learning and recognising words
Language	'Happy', 'sad', 'angry', 'nervous', 'mad', 'surprised'
Background knowledge	The children should know basic words related to the topic; the colours
Time	50–60 minutes
Classroom setting	(1) The children sit around a large table; (2) the children walk around the classroom
Materials	Large paper bags, several pairs of scissors, glue, pieces of coloured paper, a set of crayons
Age	6 and above
Level	Elementary–intermediate
Purpose	Getting familiar with vocabulary of 'feelings'

Preparation

Collect a large number of big paper bags (as many as the number of children in your classroom). Make two holes for eyes in each paper bag.

In class

1. Arrange the children around a large table. Show the bags to the children and give them one each. Keep one for yourself. Tell the children that you have to decorate the bags in order to make 'faces' that show how they feel.

    Put the material that you need in the middle of the table. Give them instructions in the L2. Help them understand the meaning of your instructions by doing what you want them to do. Use the paper bag that you have kept for yourself.

Say the following instructions and add more if you want to.

Let's colour around the eyes.
Let's draw the nose.
Let's colour the nose.
. . . and now the cheeks . . . let's colour the cheeks. What colour? Red? Or
   pink?
Let's make the hair . . . let's use these strips of paper.
Let's glue the hair on top of the head.

Let the children pick up the material they need to make their drawings. They
are free to choose the colours they want for their faces. When they are ready, say

Now let's draw the mouth.

At this point draw on the blackboard those specific features that show — by drawing
the mouth — the feelings on a face (e.g. happy, sad, surprised, crazy, etc.) Tell
the children to choose the one they like and draw it on their bag faces.

2. When the paper-bag faces are ready, ask the children to talk about the feelings
    that each of them represents; for example:

    This face is happy.
    This face is sad.
    etc.

Invite the children to put the bags on their heads (you do it, too), give each of
them a name according to the bag face that they have on (e.g. Mr Happy, Miss
Nervous, Mr Crazy, etc.).
    Walk around the classroom with the children and greet each other:

    Good morning, Mr Sad.
    Good morning, Miss Surprised.
    Hello, Miss Happy.
    etc.

3. Stick the bag faces on the wall and use them again now and then to review vocabulary and for fun.

Variations

Expand

While the children are walking and greeting each other around the classroom with their paper-bag faces on, encourage them to exchange a few expressions that may make up a dialogue.

Links

You may link this activity with: **Nicknames (11)**; **Listen and draw (48)**; **The 'ME' poster (51)**.

Teacher's diary

How much did the children enjoy this activity? Were they able to prepare the paper-bag faces? Did they follow your instructions easily while they were making them up? Did they pick up the words related to feelings easily?

---

32 What's missing?

Activity type	Learning and recognising words
Language	Words related to the pictures that you bring into the classroom
Background knowledge	The children should know how to name the objects in the pictures
Time	20 minutes
Classroom setting	Any
Materials	A set of pictures, cut from magazines, that show various objects; blu-tack
Age	6 and above
Level	Elementary—intermediate
Purpose	Increasing observation skills; reviewing vocabulary

Preparation

Prepare a set of pictures of objects that the children can name in the L2.

In class

1. Stick the pictures on the wall (or blackboard), then ask the children to name the objects that are in the pictures. Provide any words they do not remember.

2. Write on the blackboard:

   What's missing?

   Explain to them what this expression means if they do not know it. Say to the children:

Bend your head and close your eyes.

Wait for all of them to do it. Make sure that nobody cheats. Remove one picture. Say:

Now open your eyes and look. What's missing?

The children open their eyes and try to guess which object is missing.

After two or three rounds, ask one child to take your role and lead the game. Let other children do the same if they want to.

Variations

Make it difficult

Ask the children to close their eyes. Move the pictures around. Tell the children: 'Now open your eyes and look. What's changed?' The children will say expressions like the following: 'The watch was on the right of the _____. Now it's on the left of the _____.'

Links

You may link this activity with: **The micro-cities (26)**; **Shape in, shape out (58)**.

Teacher's diary

Did the children like this activity? How did they do? Did they remember the names of the objects easily?

33 1−2−3−4 . . . FREEZE!

Activity type	Counting
Language	Numbers, 'freeze'
Background knowledge	Numbers
Time	20−25 minutes
Classroom setting	Children standing in a line and facing the leader
Age	6−11
Level	Beginner and elementary
Purpose	Counting; recognising the word 'freeze'

Preparation

Tell your students that this is a popular game played in many places by six- to eight-year-old children.

In class

(The leader) Choose a child-leader. Tell the child to face the wall. While facing the wall the child counts:

> 1−2−3−4 FREEZE!,
> 5−6−7−8 FREEZE!,
> 9−10−11−12 FREEZE!,
> etc.

Every time he says 'FREEZE' he turns around towards the other children and checks if anyone is moving. The children 'caught' in movement must go back to the starting position.

(The other children) While the leader is counting the children are free to walk towards the leader but they *must* stop when they hear the word 'FREEZE'. The aim of the children is to reach the leader's position or — with larger groups — the wall where the leader is standing. The child who is the first to reach the wall gets the leader's role and has the right to start the game all over again.

Variations

Make it difficult

While the children are playing, use the following expressions to provide them with some new language:

He was moving!
Out!
You are out!
He is out!
Next turn, sorry!
You play next turn!
Who's the leader now?
I'm the leader now.

Encourage them to use these expressions.

Links

You may link this activity with: **Follow the leader (6)**.

Teacher's diary

How many numbers could the leaders count up to? Did any of them use spontaneously the expressions of encouragement that you used (Variations)?

34 Hopscotch

Topic	Numbers, days of the week or any other chosen by you
Activity type	Playing with words
Language	Words related to the topic
Background knowledge	The children should have a basic knowledge of the words that they are going to practise
Time	35—40 minutes
Classroom setting	Children in the playground or in the classroom (desks to the sides)
Materials	A piece of chalk
Age	6 and above
Level	Elementary—intermediate
Purpose	Reviewing vocabulary related to topics previously introduced

Preparation

Ask the children if they have ever played 'hopscotch' (use the equivalent word in their mother tongue). Ask them the rules of this game or, if nobody knows the game, show the rules to them.

Inform them that this is a very old game played by children in several countries around the world. In each country, rules change slightly but the game is basically the same. This time they will follow 'classroom rules'.

In class

Draw the outline on the floor. Follow the example shown in the drawing. Ask them to choose what to write in each square. Suggest to them:

Numbers.

or:

The days of the week.
Months.
Seasons.
Animals.
Colours (they colour the squares).

or:

Any words.

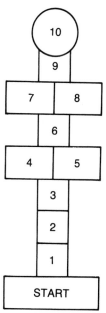

Write the set of words that they have chosen in the outline.

The children, in turn, jump in the squares on one leg. While jumping they have to say the word, number or colour they are jumping on — without looking at it. If they make a mistake — wrong word or wrong pronunciation — say:

Stop, go back and start again.

They have to go back and start the game all over again while the other children give some help by whispering the appropriate word. The best 'hopscotch jumpers' are the ones who jump and say the words without any 'stop and go back'.

When the children do not make many mistakes, change the words in the squares. This will prevent repetitiveness that may reduce motivation.

Variations

Make it difficult

Ask different groups of children, in turn, to write the words in the outline.

Links

You may link this activity with: **Let's pretend we are weather forecasters (27)**; **Let's pretend we are animals (28)**; **Class routines: Date, weather, time, the register (35)**; **Colour game: primary and secondary colours (47)**.

Teacher's diary

Did the children find the activity lively? Did they enjoy it? Did they find it was a nice way to revise English words? Have they asked you to play the game again another day?

SECTION III

EDUCATIONAL ACTIVITIES

35 Date, weather, time, the register

Topic	Class routines
Activity type	Class routines
Language	Expressions and words related to the topic
Background knowledge	Days of the week, months, how to tell the time
Time	5 minutes
Classroom setting	Any
Age	8 and above
Level	Elementary
Purpose	Gaining confidence in using language involved in daily class routines

In class

When the English class begins ask a child to call out names for the register, tell the date and the time, and make a brief report about the weather of the day. Call a different child every lesson.

This simple activity helps the children build up confidence in using the language. The more frequently they do these routines the faster they perform.

The activity may also seem obvious to you but — remember — the 'obvious' is what 'we teachers' often forget to do.

Links

You may link this activity with: **The 'ME' sign-board (10); Let's pretend we are weather forecasters (27); Hopscotch (34); Make your own calendar (36); Instructions (37); The classroom dictionary (45).**

36 Make your own calendar

Topic	Dates
Activity type	Class routines
Language	'It's . . .'
Background knowledge	Days of the week, months, seasons
Time	40–45 minutes
Classroom setting	Any (steps 1 and 3); children in a circle (step 2)
Materials	A white poster, a set of thirty-one small square cards, a set of twelve small rectangular cards, blu-tack
Age	8 and above
Level	Elementary
Purpose	Getting to know the months of the year; learning how to tell the date

Preparation

Teach words related to seasons, months and days of the week. Teach also ordinal numbers. Do it in two different lessons if you think too many words will 'crowd' the children's minds. Play the 'rhythmic game' to help them remember the words (see 'Rap the words' (activity 52)).

In class

1. Arrange the children in a circle. Ask two of them to 'mime' a month. The others guess what month it is; for example:

One child pretends to be swimming, the other pretends to be playing with the sand → beach/August.

One child pretends to be a large tree, the other one pretends to be an angel → Christmas/December.

One child pretends to throw books away, the other one jumps happily → end of school/June.

2. Get the sheet of paper. Draw a big rectangle on it following the example given here. Divide it into days and get the children to write the days of the week at the top of the columns.

3. Get the twelve rectangular cards. Ask the children to write the names of the months on them. (Write the names on the blackboard if necessary.)

4. Get the square cards. Ask the children to write the numbers from 1 to 31 on them. Now the calendar is ready.

5. Say:

    Today is Monday the 8th of October.

    Pick up the number 8 card and the month October card. Stick them on the calendar in the appropriate place. Ask the children to repeat.

6. Fill in the calendar with all the numbers (make the task easy (numbers only) or more difficult), asking 'What is the date tomorrow/the day after tomorrow?', 'What was the date yesterday/on Saturday?' Tell the children that saying the date is a 'class routine': they, in turn, will do it at the beginning of each lesson, and put up the appropriate cards.

Variations

Expand

Ask the children to make a drawing of each season. They write a short paragraph about the seasons; for example, 'Spring is warm, Summer is hot, Autumn is windy, Winter is snowy.' They can expand their paragraphs, depending on their proficiency.

Links

You may link this activity with: **Let's pretend we are weather forecasters (27)**; **Class routines: Date, weather, time, the register (35)**; **Rap the words (52)**.

Teacher's diary

Did the children like building up their own calendar? Was it too complicated for you to prepare the cards? If yes, how can you make it simple? Do the children find it useful to have the calendar? Can they tell the date easily? Do they usually check how many English lessons they have had in a month?

			OCTOBER			
MONDAY	TUESDAY	WEDNESDAY	THURSDAY	FRIDAY	SATURDAY	SUNDAY
	3	4				

37   Instructions

Topic	Classroom instructions
Activity type	Class routines
Language	Words related to the topic
Time	40–50 minutes
Classroom setting	Any
Materials	A set of white (or coloured) sheets of paper, crayons, a set of white flashcards, blu-tack
Age	7 and above
Level	Elementary
Purpose	Getting to know classroom instructions

In class

1. **(In L1)** Ask the children what the word 'instructions' means to them. Elicit answers and give your examples.

2. Hand out the set of sheets of paper to the children. Ask the children to draw pictures of the things they usually do at school. When they have finished, collect the drawings and stick them on the blackboard. Point at each drawing and say the appropriate instruction for it; for example, if the picture shows a crayon, say 'Colour', if the picture shows a pen, say 'Write', etc.

3. Review the instructions orally by asking the children to point to the appropriate picture when you say the instruction.

4. Write the instructions on the blackboard next to each drawing. Help the children read them.

5. Put the pictures on the wall with the help of the children. Give them the set of blank flashcards. Ask them to copy the instructions from the blackboard (or you do it if the children are too young). When the flashcards are ready with the instructions written on them, the children match them with the appropriate drawings and stick them on the wall next to the appropriate pictures for future reviewing.

Links

You may link this activity with: **Class routines: Date, weather, time, the register (35)**.

Teacher's diary

Can the children remember the instructions easily? Do they use these instructions when talking to each other?

---

38 The 'moving letter'

Topic	The alphabet
Activity type	Playing with the alphabet
Language	'It's a/an _____'; the letters of the alphabet; 'He's making a _____'
Background knowledge	The alphabet
Time	15−20 minutes
Classroom setting	Children standing in a circle
Materials	None
Age	6−11
Level	Beginner−elementary
Purpose	Getting familiar with the letters of the alphabet

In class

Tell the children to stand in a circle. One child goes to the centre of the circle. Ask him to think of a letter of the alphabet. He has to move around in small steps as if he were following the shape of a letter. The other children have to recognise which letter it is and report it to the rest of the class using one of the following two expressions:

[letter]
It's a/an [letter].

When the children are getting familiar with the game, introduce the expression

He's making a/an [letter].

Do not force them to use one or the other expression at any stage. In fact, the children should eventually be free to use the expression they feel more comfortable with.

Give each child the chance to be the 'moving letter' at least once.

Links

You may link this activity with: **Letter shape (39)**; **Alphabet line (40)**.

Teacher's diary

Did the activity help the children recall the letters of the alphabet more easily?

---

39 Letter shape

Topic	The alphabet
Activity type	Playing with the alphabet
Language	'It's a/an [letter]'
Background knowledge	The alphabet
Time	15−20 minutes
Classroom setting	Children standing in the middle of the room in groups of 7/8
Materials	None
Age	7−11
Level	Beginner−elementary
Purpose	Getting familiar with the letters of the alphabet

In class

Tell your students to move to the centre of the room. Divide them into groups of seven or eight. Tell each group to choose a 'secret' letter. In turn, the groups rush to the centre and lie down on the floor in the shape of the 'secret' letter. The other groups have to recognise the letter and report it using one of the following expressions:

    [letter]
    It's a/an [letter].

If some groups perform in a messy way, introduce the expression of complaint that the reporters may need to use:

    But that's not a 'B', it's a 'D'.

The number of groups to make up depends on the number of children that you have in your group. Allow each group to have enough children. This helps them to form larger and clearer letters. Even two groups are enough. Encourage the children to play this game in a 'real rush' to create a lively atmosphere. Suggest they wear comfortable clothes when they play this game.

Links

You may link this activity with: **The 'moving letter' (38)**; **Alphabet line (40)**.

Teacher's diary

Was the activity a little bit messy? Did it help the children recall the letters of the alphabet more easily?

---

40 Alphabet line

Topic	The alphabet
Activity type	Playing with the alphabet
Language	Letters and words
Background knowledge	The alphabet
Time	50—60 minutes
Classroom setting	Children sitting in a circle
Materials	A rope or a string, 26 clothes pegs, a collection of real things or pictures of things for each letter, 26 pieces of paper, blu-tack
Age	7 and above
Level	Elementary
Purpose	Getting familiar with the letters of the alphabet; matching letters with the beginning of words; reviewing and increasing vocabulary

Preparation

Write each letter of the alphabet on a separate piece of paper. If possible, do it with the help of the children.

In class

1. Lay the pieces of paper with the letters written on them on the floor in random order. Ask a few children to put the clothes pegs on the line. Ask:

Can you hang up the letters of the alphabet in the right order?

Let the children pick up the letters and hang them on the line all together. Encourage them to name the letters while hanging them up.

2. Look for real things or pictures to hang from each clothes peg. Point out the matching of letter and beginning of word. Say:

The name of this letter is B. It sounds like 'ba': 'balloon'.

Hang the balloon from the appropriate clothes peg. (The letter should still be there.) Ask the children to help you in the search. Say:

Can you help me find an object for the letter C?

Let them guess names of things while they are searching. Accept nonsense names by saying:

This is fun. But it's not the right one.

Then provide the correct name.

Stop hanging objects from the clothes line when you realise that the children have run out of words to suggest.

3. Let the children repeat the names of the objects hanging from the clothes line. Then collect the letters and use them to spell some of the words the children have just learned (be ready to have a few extra letters for doubles).

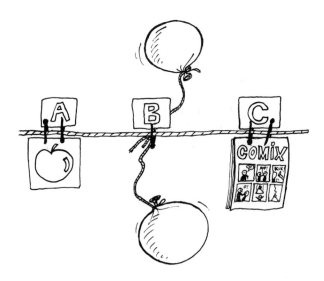

Variations

Expand

Encourage them to note down the words in their folder now that they can see them in the written form. Suggest they draw an appropriate picture next to each word to show the meaning.

Do not show the spelling of all the words. It is too boring for children to see the written form of many words in just one day. Their attention span may easily fade. Focus, therefore, only on the ones the children have shown they remember better.

Links

You may link this activity with: **The 'moving letter' (38)**; **Letter shape (39)**.

Teacher's diary

Did the activity help the children learn a large number of words? What can you do to make them remember these words easily?

41   A birthday gift

Topic   Birthday gifts

Activity type   Playing with words

Language   Words related to the topic

Background   The children need to know basic words related to the topic
knowledge

Time   15–20 minutes

Classroom   Children sitting in a circle on the floor
setting

Materials   A ball

Age   8 and above

Level   Elementary–intermediate

Purpose   Searching for and using vocabulary

In class

1. Every time it is a child's birthday invite the classmates to sing the 'Happy Birthday' song.

2. Let the children sit down on the floor in a circle. Tell them to think of an object that they wish to give to their friend as a birthday gift. Be ready to provide L2 words if the children need them. The classroom dictionary will help you with that.

3. Get the ball. Throw the ball to the children. The one who gets it says the object she would like to give as a gift (e.g. a video-game machine) to her friend. Then she throws the ball to another child who does the same. This goes on for a few minutes until all the children have no more gifts (words) to give to their classmate.

Links

You may link this activity with the activities in Section I; **Halloween (64)**.

42 The dictionary poster

Topic	Vocabulary
Activity type	Playing with words
Language	Words the children have come across
Background knowledge	As in Language
Time	A few minutes any time the children feel ready for it
Classroom setting	Any
Materials	A large piece of paper
Age	7 and above
Level	Elementary and above
Purpose	Playing with words; reviewing vocabulary; thinking about the sound and meaning of words

In class

1. Bring a big sheet of paper (any colour), stick it on the wall and write 'Our dictionary poster' on it. Tell the children that they are free to use the poster to write any words or expressions any time they feel like it. Suggest to them reasons why they may decide to write a word:

    They like the word very much because of the meaning.
    They like the sound of the word.
    They do not like it because it is too difficult to remember.
    It was the first word they learned.

    Tell them that they can have any other personal reasons to write their words. Let them use any colour, shape and size when they write the words. The more crowded, coloured and funny the poster is, the more enjoyable it is to look at it.

2. When the poster is ready — after a few days (or weeks) — ask the children to read the words they have written down previously. Tell them to say the meaning. If they have too many words (or new words) to write, add other posters — the more posters you have in class the better it is for reminding the children of vocabulary.

Variations

Expand

Ask the children to make up sentences with the words that they find on the poster.

Links

You may link this activity with: **L2 borrowing game (21)**; **Let's pretend we are weather forecasters (27)**; **The hungriest poster (46)**; **Rap the words (52)**; **Search for the English word (57)**.

Teacher's diary

How many posters did the children ask to prepare? Do you often use these posters as a way of referring to vocabulary?

---

43 If I . . .

Topic	Background noise
Activity type	Learning and recognising words
Language	Words related to the topic
Time	15–20 minutes
Classroom setting	Any
Age	7 and above
Level	Elementary and above
Purpose	Searching for sounds; searching for and using vocabulary

In class

1. Write on the blackboard:

    . . . keep silent . . .

    ask the children for the meaning since they may already know it.
    Write next:

    . . . what do I hear?

    explain the meaning. Write in front of the words:

    If I . . .

    explain the meaning (L1 allowed) to the children.
    Now the sentence on the blackboard is:

    If I keep silent what do I hear?

2. Tell the children to close their eyes, listen carefully to all the sounds inside and
    outside the classroom. Create an atmosphere of complete silence in the classroom

and give the children a few seconds (50—60) to accomplish their task. When the seconds are over, ask the children to go to the blackboard and make a drawing of the sounds they heard; for example:

> a child crying outside, a motorbike going by, a car engine starting, a door slammed by someone, a pen falling on the floor, a child yawning loudly, someone laughing, etc.

When they have completed their drawings teach them the appropriate words.

At earlier stages (first year of L2 instruction) teach just the words related to the objects or people making the actions; for example:

> a child, a car, a door, etc.

Variations

Make it difficult

At later stages teach the words related to the objects and the actions; for example:

> a child crying outside, a car engine starting, etc.

Introduce the words orally first, then teach the written forms by writing them under the appropriate drawings.

Links

You may link this activity with: **The classroom band (53)**.

Teacher's diary

How much new vocabulary have you been able to teach? Did the children enjoy learning new words in this way?

---

44 Extra cards? Put them in the pocket

Topic	Varied
Activity type	Learning and recognising words
Language	Words related to the topic
Background knowledge	The children should already have internalised the words related to the topic
Time	10–20 minutes
Classroom setting	Any
Materials	A large sheet of paper, a set of small sheets of cards, a pair of scissors, glue, markers
Age	8 and above
Level	Elementary and above
Purpose	Reviewing familiar vocabulary

Preparation

Prepare a large colourful poster together with the children. Apply eight to ten paper pockets (or use envelopes) by pasting them on it. Stick the poster on the wall and keep it ready to be filled up during your activities.

In class

1. When the walls are full of word labels and pictures and you want to renew them, check which set of labels has been up on the wall for a long time. Check if the children remember the words that you want to remove. If they do, ask them what

name they want to give to the set; for example, food, clothes, shapes, sports, etc. They write this name at the top of a pocket and put the cards in it.

Variations

Expand

Every now and then play a quick lexical game, during which the children check if they still remember the meaning of the words. They may do it in one of the following ways:

> Miming the meaning.
> Making up sentences in which the words have been used appropriately.
> Translating the words into the L1.

Links

You may link this activity with: **Class labels (68)**.

Teacher's diary

How useful is this pocket poster? Is it good reference for the children? Do they often use it to revise familiar vocabulary?

---

45 The classroom dictionary

Topic	Varied
Activity type	Learning and recognising words
Language	Words related to the topic
Time	5–10 minutes
Classroom setting	Any
Materials	A bilingual dictionary
Age	6 and above
Level	Elementary and above
Purpose	Searching for new words; learning how to use a dictionary

In class

When you need a new word or phrase and you do not know it, do not get discouraged. Remember that sometimes it is natural not to know a word. Bring an English/English dictionary to class and simply tell the children that you need to use it sometimes. It will be nice to learn words together.

If the children are at the beginning of their school instruction, get the dictionary, check the word and give the appropriate translation.

At later stages, encourage the children to start checking the dictionary by themselves. Give them any information they may need in order to do this. When possible, use English/English or bilingual dictionaries appropriate to your learners' age and study skills ability. So, keep in your classroom two (if not more) dictionaries that you will call: the 'teacher's dictionary' (the more detailed one) and 'the children's dictionary' (the simple one).

Variations

Expand

Help grown-up learners (twelve—thirteen years old) with the major details that they need to know in order to use the dictionary effectively.

Links

You may link this activity with: **Class routines: Date, weather, time, the register (35)**.

Teacher's diary

How often do you use the classroom dictionary? Is it useful? How frequently do the children ask to use the picture dictionaries?

---

46 The hungriest poster

Topic	Food
Activity type	Learning and recognising words
Language	Focus on words related to food
Time	50−60 minutes
Classroom setting	Groups of 3/5
Materials	A large sheet of paper per group, crayons, pencils; a set of cut-outs of food from magazines, etc.
Age	7 and above
Level	Elementary and above
Purpose	Learning 'food' vocabulary

Preparation

Prepare a set of cut-outs of 'food'.

In class

1. **(In L1)** Ask the children what English words related to food they already know. If they cannot think of any, help them. Write their suggestions on the blackboard. Let them read the words you have elicited from them.

2. Show the cut-outs and teach some new words through them.

3. Divide the children into groups of three to five according to the number of students you have in the class. Give them the sheets of paper.
   Ask the groups to make a drawing of a huge sandwich to give to the 'hungriest person'. Let the groups make their own choice but give suggestions if necessary. Help them with the drawings.

4. Provide the words for the food that they are drawing. Help them write these new words on the poster.

5. When the sandwiches are ready, each group shows its own to the class. Each group points out the new words they have come across. The children decide which is the 'hungriest poster'. Finally, the children stick the posters on the wall.

Variations

Change topic

Ask the children to make up 'The thirstiest poster' (use drinks instead of food) or 'The fullest wardrobe' using clothes.

Links

You may link this activity with: **The dictionary poster (42)**.

Teacher's diary

How much did the children enjoy this activity? How often do they look at these posters as a vocabulary reference for the topic 'Food'?

---

47 Colour game: primary and secondary colours

Topic	Primary and secondary colours
Activity type	Learning and recognising words
Language	Words related to colours
Time	30–40 minutes
Classroom setting	Any
Materials	Two similar sets of coloured flashcards, blu-tack
Age	7 and above
Level	Elementary
Purpose	Learning about primary and secondary colours; getting familiar with vocabulary related to 'colours'

In class

1. **(In L1)** Introduce the topic by making the children aware of the difference between primary and secondary colours.

    (In L2) Stick the first set of flashcards on the wall with the blu-tack and show the children which colours are to be combined to get a third one. Say:

    If you mix *blue* and *red* you get *purple*.

    Or

    Yellow and *blue* gives *green*.

    Point to the flashcards when you say the names of colours. Ask the children to repeat these names.

2. When the children have become familiar with the new words, remove the flashcards from the wall and put them on a desk at random. Put the second set of flashcards on another desk at random. Divide the children into two groups. Give each group a set of flashcards. The two groups select the cards and stick them on the wall, matching them in order to make the secondary colours. They should do it as quickly as possible, without mixing up the cards. Finally, the groups in turn tell what colours they have made.

3. Write the names of the colours on the blackboard. Ask the children to read the words.

Variations

Expand

Dictate how secondary colours are made. The children reproduce them in their folders. At the end, they write the names of the colours under their drawings.

Links

You may link this activity with: **Hopscotch (34)**; **Footcolour (49)**; **The 'ME' poster (51)**.

Teacher's diary

Did the children already know how to mix colours? Did they enjoy learning it in English?

---

48 Listen and draw

Topic	Music and feelings
Activity type	Learning and recognising words
Language	Simple words related to feelings
Time	20 minutes
Classroom setting	Any
Materials	A tape-recorder; a cassette with a piece of music selected by you; three labels: 'HAPPY', 'SAD', 'INDIFFERENT'. Also, each child needs a piece of paper, a pencil, crayons
Age	7 and above
Level	Elementary
Purpose	Relating music to feelings; learning basic vocabulary related to 'feelings'

In class

1. **(In L1)** Introduce a piece of music. Talk briefly about the composer or group. Tell the children what kind of music they will be listening to.

   Ask them to get a piece of paper, their pencil and crayons. Tell them to draw something — whatever they like — while listening to the music.

2. **(In L2)** When the children are ready with their drawings take a look at them and make comments by saying:

   Good. That is nice. I like it. Wonderful.

   or

   A little bit messy!

Ask for brief descriptions of the drawings — L1 admitted.

Prepare the three labels, 'HAPPY', 'SAD', 'INDIFFERENT', and stick them on the wall. Show the three labels, explain the meanings, ask the children to stick their drawings under the appropriate label, according to the feeling that the music has created in them.

Variations

Make it difficult

Ask the children to produce sentences like the following: 'I feel happy because I like this piece of music', 'I feel sad because I don't like it', etc.

Links

You may link this activity with: **Paper-bag faces (31)**.

Teacher's diary

How did the children do in this activity? Did they enjoy listening to music? Were they aware of their feelings?

49 Footcolour

Topic	Colours
Activity type	Expressing opinions
Language	Simple words related to colours
Background knowledge	The children should know expression such as: 'I like ...'/ 'My favourite colour is ...'
Time	40—50 minutes
Classroom setting	In the playground or in a large space
Materials	The largest piece of paper you can find or several large pieces of paper; large jars* of non-toxic paint; a bowl; soap; a few towels
Age	6—11
Level	Elementary—intermediate
Purpose	Having fun while messing around; reinforcing how to express opinions

Preparation

Review the expressions that the children need to use when they want to express opinions (see below).

In class

Wait for a warm day. Go to an outside area with the children (or make as much space

---

*These should be as large as a child's foot in order to give the child the chance to dip his or her foot inside.

as you can in your classroom). Bring the papers and jars with you. The children will help you. Spread the papers on the floor. Put the jars near them. Tell the children:

Now we are going to paint with our feet.

Say:

Take your shoes off.

Wait for them to do it and put the shoes in one corner. If possible, you do it, too, to help them understand your command. Say:

Now, take your socks off.

Say:

I like blue.

Dip one of your feet or both into the jar containing the blue paint and walk on the papers. Look at the children and — with a smile — invite them to do the same. When the children dip their feet in the boxes encourage them to say the expressions:

I like red.
My favourite colour is purple.
I love blue!
Look, yellow!
My feet are yellow!
I can walk on yellow!

Repeat these expressions yourself several times. Allow the children to dip in the boxes more than once if they like more colours. If the children crowd around the boxes too wildly, ask them to take turns.

When the footcolour posters are ready, say:

Now we wash one by one. Stand in a line!

Get the bowl, wash your feet first, then help the children to do the same. Invite the children, if necessary, to be patient for the 'washing' turn. Let the poster (or posters) dry. Then hang it (them) on the wall. Ask the children to recognise their work and say:

This is mine!
This is my foot!
This red foot is mine because I like red.

Variations

Change this activity into a 'handcolour' poster if you find it hard to do what I have described above. The procedure and language input are the same but this time display the drawing paper on the wall and ask the children to use their hands instead of their feet.

Links

You may link this activity with: **Colour game: primary and secondary colours (47)**.

Teacher's diary

Was it difficult to perform this activity? Did it become too messy? How much language did the children spontaneously produce?

---

50 The touch and feel book: make your own

Topic   Tactile feelings

Activity type   Describing

Language   Descriptive adjectives

Background knowledge   The children should know the names of the objects that are described in this activity

Time   Two periods of 50/60 minutes

Classroom setting   Any

Materials   Larger photocopies of the drawings provided here; 9 sheets of white paper; large photocopies of the expressions provided here. Also glue, a pair of scissors, a piece of fur, a piece of wood, a sponge, some sandpaper, a glass, a piece of plastic (small piece of OHP transparency is ideal), a ball on the end of a rubber band, a feather

Age   6 and above

Level   Intermediate

Purpose   Learning how to describe objects

Preparation

Photocopy* the drawings provided for you on page 130. Photocopy* the descriptions of the drawings provided for you on page 129. Make enlargements of each drawing

*You are permitted to photocopy these pages for classroom use.

to make sure that all the children will be able to see them well. At home, select the objects listed above (unless you have them already at school) and bring them to school.

In class

1. Display the objects on a table. Review the name of each object by asking:

    Do you remember what this is?

2. Introduce the concept of 'Touch and feel'. Touch the objects one by one and say slowly:

soft	(fur)
hard	(wood)
spongy	(sponge)
scratchy	(sandpaper)
cool and smooth	(glass)
smooth	(plastic)
stretchy	(rubber band)
ticklish	(feather)

    Invite the children to touch the objects to get the feelings. Encourage them to repeat the adjectives while they touch. Provide the translation into L1 for those adjectives that the children find difficult to understand.

3. Get the drawings and show them to the children. Say:

    Now we make our book.

    Ask them to match the objects with the drawings. When the matching is completed, ask them to 'cut' the objects and 'paste' them onto the pages (except for the glass, a piece of transparent plastic in the shape of a glass can replace it!). The objects will obviously be shaped to fit the drawings. While the children 'cut and paste', say and encourage them to say expressions like:

    The feather goes here.
    . . . and the sponge goes there.
    . . . too big! Cut it.
    Get the glue.
    Too much glue. Less next time!
    Careful!
    Here it goes. Good job!

4. When the drawings are ready, get the nine sheets of white paper. Read the descriptions provided for you on page 129. While reading, stress the adjectives.
    Ask the children to find the appropriate drawing for each description. Stick

each 'description' on a white sheet of paper and put the drawing next to it. Let the children help you do it.

5. Arrange all the papers in a book format, following this example:

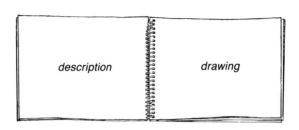

Bind them. Prepare a cover which says:

> *The touch and feel book*
>   by . . . . .

6. Ask the children to go through the book, colour the drawings — they may do it in turn — and highlight the adjectives that describe the objects.
    Now the book is ready to be read to and by the children.

Links

You may link this activity with: **Bubbles search (75)**; **If walls talk you read them (76)**; **Book 'n' balloons (77)**; **Your story, my writing (78)**; **A noisy story, a noisy picture (79)**; **A quiet story, a quiet picture (80)**; **Shall we read a fairy-tale? (81)**.

Teacher's diary

Was the preparation for this activity too complicated for you? How did the children do? Were they able to make up the book? How much new language did they learn? Will the book help them remember the new language more easily?

What feels soft?
Fur is soft like a puppy,
like a kitten . . . all furry.
Fur feels warm and soft.

Wood is hard.
Feel the table.
Isn't it hard?
Wood always feels hard!

A sponge is spongy!
Soft and squishy,
squashy, squishy.
A sponge is spongy!
Feel it!
Press it!
Squeeze it!

Sand is scratchy!
Warm-in-the-sun sand!
Sand between your toes!
Feel the scratchy sand.

A glass is smooth!
Plastic is clear and smooth!
Cool and smooth
when you touch it!
Feel it!
Look through it!
You can see the other side!

Rubber is stretchy!
Pull it. Stretch it!
It bounces back!
Feel the bouncy rubber
band!

What is ticklish? Feathers are
ticklish. Feel it with your nose.
Isn't it fun to TOUCH and FEEL?

51 The 'ME' poster

Topic	Physical features
Activity type	Describing
Language	Focus on words related to physical features
Background knowledge	The children should know the basic words related to colours
Time	Two periods of 45/50 minutes
Classroom setting	The classroom should be empty of desks
Materials	Large pieces of paper — as many as the number of children you have in your group and as big as a child's body — scissors, crayons
Age	9 and above
Level	Elementary—intermediate
Purpose	Learning how to describe physical features

In class

1. Place half the number of papers you have on the floor (say twelve). Ask twelve children to lie down on the papers. Ask the other children to choose a partner and trace the outline of the partner's body with a crayon or a pencil. Now place the other twelve sheets of paper on the floor. Now the children who lay down first trace the body for the others.

2. When the tracing is completed, the children colour their own 'portraits' according to their own physical features. While they are doing it, teach the appropriate words:

   blond hair   brown eyes   large nose

brown hair	black eyes	small nose
black hair	blue eyes	large mouth
red hair	green eyes	small mouth
short hair	big eyes	big hands
long hair	small eyes	small hands
curly hair		short legs
		long legs

and others that may spontaneously come up.

When the portraits have been completed, the children cut them out and hang the portraits on the wall.

3. The children, in turn, describe each other's portrait, for example:

Maria has brown hair, black eyes, a large nose and long legs.

At a complete beginner level, encourage (and accept!) the children to use just words, for example:

Maria — blond hair — black eyes — large nose — long legs.
Giuseppe — curly hair — black hair — large mouth — brown eyes — short legs.

Variations

Expand

Write the descriptive phrases on the blackboard. Invite the children to read them aloud. Ask them to recognise which phrases refer to their own physical features. They copy these phrases on their personal portrait.

Links

You may link this activity with: **Paper-bag faces (31)**; **Colour game: primary and secondary colours (47)**; **A day in the life of ... (63)**.

Teacher's diary

Did the activity last the time that you had planned? Did the children like it? Can they now make a simple description of a friend?

---

52 Rap the words

Topic	Any chosen by you
Activity type	Playing with words
Language	Words related to the topic
Time	10–15 minutes
Classroom setting	Any
Materials	(Optional) a cassette-recorder, an audio-cassette with a piece of rhythmic music
Age	6 and above
Level	Beginner and above
Purpose	Helping children retain vocabulary

In class

1. Introduce the words* orally using pictures, drawings or any other technique appropriate for vocabulary teaching.

2. Give the children a chance to repeat the words together with you with the aim of doing the following:

   • Practising appropriate pronunciation.

   • 'Studying' the items to remember them more easily.

   Put the 'rhythmic' piece of music in the background — or use a relaxed friendly rhythm yourself similar to a rap sound — and repeat the list of words together with the children while following the rhythm. When they feel confident in saying the words, keep silent and make them repeat the words rhythmically by themselves.

   *For example, the months of the year, the seasons, the days of the week, animals, toys.

Variations

Make it difficult

The students make up sentences with the words. They read the sentences following the rhythmic sounds.

Links

You may link this activity with: **Make your own calendar (36)**; **The dictionary poster (42)** or any other activity that introduces a new set of words.

Teacher's diary

Did the children enjoy repeating lists of words in this way? Do you think this will encourage them to do it more often? Will this help them remember the words more easily?

---

53 The classroom band

Topic	Musical instruments
Activity type	Learning and recognising words
Language	Words related to the topic; 'Who's got?'; 'Can I hear ...?'
Time	25–30 minutes
Classroom setting	Any
Materials	A cassette with pieces of music; a set of pictures of instruments or an OHP transparency with the silhouettes of instruments; a set of flashcards with the names of the instruments; any kind of object that can be used as an instrument
Age	6 and above
Level	Beginner and elementary
Purpose	Learning words related to musical instruments; having fun with these instruments

Preparation

1. Prepare an audio-cassette with a series of short pieces of music in which the musical instruments are easily recognisable.

2. Collect a set of pictures of instruments and a set of flashcards with the names of the instruments written on them.

   As an alternative, and if you have an overhead projector available in your school, prepare a transparency with clear silhouettes of instruments and a second transparency with the names of the instruments written on it.

3. Tell the children to bring from home any objects that they think can be used as

an instrument; for example, a few pot lids, empty jugs, round paper boxes, metal spoons, small containers with rice inside, etc.

In class

1. **(In L1)**   Collect the objects that the children have brought from home. Ask them what kind of instruments each of them reminds them of.

2. Play the cassette and ask the children what instruments they can recognise.

3. **(In L2)**   Show the pictures (or silhouettes) and teach the names of the instruments. When the children have become familiar with these new words, say:

    Now let's make our classroom band.

    Give each child an object. Let them decide which instrument each object is going to be. Ask:

    'Who's got a trumpet?', 'Who's got a drum?'
    etc.

    Accept answers like hands up, 'Me', or, at later stages, 'I've got a drum.'
        As an alternative, ask 'Who plays the trumpet?', 'Who plays the drum?' Once again, accept answers like hands up, 'Me', or 'I do', 'I play the drum.' 'I play it.'

4. Let the band march around the classroom while playing their improvised instruments.

5. When the marching band is getting too noisy, ask them to put the instruments on a table. Give them the flashcards with the names of the instruments written on them. The children stick the flashcards on the appropriate instruments.

Variations

Arrange the children with their instruments in a circle. Say 'Let me hear the sound of a . . . drum.' The child who has got the drum plays it for a few moments. Continue like this until all the children have had the chance to play their 'sounds'.

Links

You may link this activity with: **Who's got the ring? (15)**; **If I . . . (43)**.

Teacher's diary

Did the children have fun? Was the activity useful to introduce new vocabulary? What other language-learning activities can be planned around the topic 'Music'?

---

54 Body movements

Topic	Body movements and body positions
Activity type	Understanding and giving directions
Language	Commands related to the topic
Time	30–40 minutes
Classroom setting	Children standing in the playground or in the classroom
Age	6 and above
Level	Elementary and above
Purpose	Giving and understanding physical commands

In class

Teach the meaning of:

> body
> forward/backward
> left/right
> line/row

Tell the children to listen carefully to your commands, watch the actions that you do to show them what they have to do and imitate you. Feel free to change the commands suggested below if you think the needs of your children differ and if you do not feel confident in performing the actions. Do not introduce all the commands in just one lesson if you believe the children's minds may become too crowded with too many words.

The children do not need to talk during the activity. They only need to show that they understand the meaning of your commands and, little by little, get familiar with them. Perform this activity several times during a term to make sure that the children are familiarised with the commands. In fact, it may take a long time before the children (or, at least, some of them) are ready to produce the commands by themselves. The following commands are the ones that the children may need to know:

stand in a line	jump
stand in a row	jump once
stand up	jump twice
swim	jump three times
do a somersault	... and now fall down
turn your body	bend down slowly
turn to the left	bend your body
turn to the right	stand on top of the chair
turn to the right and walk	stand on top of the desk
look down	jump down
look up	take three steps forward
look left	take two steps forward
look right	take one giant step
one by one	take one baby step

Variations

Make it difficult

As soon as you realise that the children are able to say the commands, ask them to be leaders and give the commands to the class.

Links

You may link this activity with: **Look, listen and move (55)**; **Classdance (56)**; **Shape in, shape out (58)**; **Blind steps (61)**.

Teacher's diary

Did the children learn to understand the commands easily? Are they ready now to say the commands? How long did it take them to learn how to say the commands?

---

55 Look, listen and move

Topic	Body movements
Activity type	Listening to a story
Language	Description of body movements
Background knowledge	Simple words related to parts of the body, e.g. 'legs', 'arms', 'feet', 'eyes', and to actions, e.g. 'jump', 'sit down', 'sleep'
Time	30–40 minutes
Classroom setting	Children standing around the classroom
Materials	Photos from magazines of children moving, playing, etc., showing a progression from activity to calm
Age	7 and above
Level	Elementary
Purpose	Understanding the description of body movements

Preparation

Display large photos or drawings of children running, jumping, sitting, sleeping, etc.

Make sure that the photos or drawings are large enough to be seen by all the children. Prepare captions such as 'I am jumping', 'I am skipping', etc.

In class

1. **(In L1)** Show the drawings to the children. Ask them what the child is doing in each picture.

2. **(In L2)** Slowly start reading each caption aloud while pointing at the pictures. Encourage the children to imitate the actions of the child in the pictures. (Do

the actions yourself; for example, 'I am jumping', 'I am walking'.) Change the rhythm of your voice according to the content of each caption; for example:

I am walking   read slowly
I am sleeping   read softly
I am running   read faster
I am jumping   read loudly

Read the captions several times until the children become familiar with them and the movements linked to them and the children are still enjoying the fun raised by the movements.

3. When this phase is finished invite the children to 'calm down', stop moving and sit down in a circle. Read out all the captions again while they look closely at the pictures — but this time let them focus on the meaning of the expressions. Present the activities in ascending or descending order of energetic activity; for example:

jumping → sleeping
sleeping → jumping

Accelerate or slow down the pace of the speaking as appropriate.
Accept translation into L1.

4. From time to time — and when the children feel like it — 'play' this activity again for vocabulary review and for pure fun!

Variations

Make it difficult

Ask the children to read the captions. Give them the pictures in jumbled order. They match pictures and captions and stick them on the wall.

Links

You may link this activity with: **Body movements (54)**; **Classdance (56)**.

Teacher's diary

Did the children enjoy moving? What expressions were they able to understand more easily? Which ones do they remember now?

56 Classdance

Topic	Body movements
Activity type	Understanding and giving directions
Language	Words related to body movements
Background knowledge	Words related to the parts of the body
Time	30—40 minutes
Classroom setting	Children standing around the classroom
Materials	An audio-cassette with pieces of music recorded on it, a cassette-recorder
Age	6 and above
Level	Elementary—intermediate
Purpose	Understanding commands

Preparation

Prepare a cassette with some pieces of music that you think the children may enjoy. Listen carefully to the music and try to think of easy physical exercises that may fit the rhythm of the music. At school announce to the children that they will have a dance class during which they will practise exercises to the music.

In class

Say:

Now we are going to dance.

Put the music on. Let the children dance freely for a few moments, then start your commands:

shake your body	bend your body
bend to your right	bend to your left
touch your toes	clap your hands
jog on your feet	jump
walk to your right	walk to your left
(1, 2, 3, 4 steps)	(1, 2, 3, 4 steps)
hands up	hands down
touch your wrist	twist your body
bend your head — pull it up	bend your head to the right
bend your head to the left	kick to the front
kick to the right	kick to the left

Do the exercises along with the children. This is the only way for them to understand the meaning at the beginning. When they perform an exercise count the times you want them to do it, following the rhythm:

... and one, two, three, four, and again two, three, four ... once again two, three, four.

Variations

Expand

Repeat the activity several times a term to give the children an opportunity to familiarise themselves with the words faster. Every time add some new commands. Make sure that you change the music every now and then to avoid repetitiveness.

Links

You may link this activity with: **Body movements (54)**; **Look, listen and move (55)**; **Blind steps (61)**.

Teacher's diary

Did the children understand the commands easily? Do they remember them when you repeat the activity? Can any of them say the commands?

---

57   Search for the English word

Topic	Sports
Activity type	Playing with words
Language	L2 words used in sports
Time	30—40 minutes
Classroom setting	Any
Materials	A large piece of paper, crayons, pencils, a set of sports headlines
Age	9 and above
Level	Elementary—intermediate
Purpose	Expanding vocabulary; recognising L2 sports words used in the L1

Preparation

Prepare a set of sports headlines cut out from sports magazines or newspapers in the children's mother tongue. Each headline should contain one or more English words. The set of English words provided below may help you in your search. These are English words that are now widely used in other languages:

baseball, basketball, crawl, corner, cross, cross-country, dive, dribbling, finish, football, game, goal, handball, hurdle, kick, match-ball, net, off-side, out, penalty, pivot, play maker, relay, rush, rugby, set, slalom, softball, skip, smash, starting blocks, spring, stopper, strike, volleyball.

In class

1. Make the children aware that a large amount of sports terminology in their L1 has been 'borrowed' from English. Ask them if they know a few words already.

2. Tell them that they will have to play a 'searching game' in order to find the English word in the headlines that you have collected. Mention a few features that may help them recognise the 'foreign' words.

Read the headlines to them slowly. If they recognise the 'word' write it on the blackboard. Ask them for the meaning or explanation (in L1, if necessary) or provide it for them if they do not know it.

Variations

Expand

When you have enough words on the blackboard, prepare a poster of 'English SPORTS words'. Invite the children to write the words on the poster by copying them from the blackboard. Then help them make drawings that show the meaning next to each word.

Links

You may link this activity with: **L2 'borrowing' game (21)**; **The dictionary poster (42)**.

Teacher's diary

Did the children already know any of these words? Did they know the meaning? Which were the ones they had come across for the first time? Were they able to recognise the words in the contexts that you had given to them?

---

58 Shape in, shape out

Topic	Shapes
Activity type	Learning and recognising words
Language	Shapes; 'jump in', 'jump out', 'stand in the', 'go', 'run'; prepositions
Background knowledge	Shapes
Time	20–30 minutes
Classroom setting	Children standing in the middle of the room in groups of 4/5
Materials	Coloured adhesive tape, cardboard cut in geometrical shapes
Age	6 and above
Level	Elementary
Purpose	Learning shapes; learning prepositions of place and movement

Preparation

Introduce the vocabulary related to shapes by using coloured cardboard cut in geometrical forms. Use also the science book or drawings made by the children.

In class

1. Tell the children to move to the centre of the room. Divide them into groups of four or five. Make big shapes on the floor by using the adhesive tape. Say:

    Now we are going to jump. Get ready.

Give each group one instruction at a time, choosing among the list given below. This is an example:

Group A, jump in the circle. Group B, jump to the left of the circle.

At the very beginning perform along with them to show the meaning of the instructions, or use gestures. Encourage them while they are performing with expressions like 'Great', 'That was good', etc.

2. When the children are ready for production, choose a child leader. Now the leader will give the instructions to the groups. Let the children rotate as leaders.
    List of suitable instructions:

Jump in the square.
Jump out of the circle.
Jump to the right/left of . . .
Stand on top of . . .
Stand at the bottom of . . .
Stand in the middle of . . .
Go/run around the . . .
Sit in the . . .

The more instructions you can think of the more enjoyable the activity is. But do not use a large set of instructions the first time you play the game. Six or eight instructions are enough in one lesson. Add a few more every time you play the game again.

Variations

Expand

Have a picture dictation. Dictate like the following examples: 'Draw a red circle', 'Draw a blue square in the red circle', 'Draw a large yellow rectangle next to the circle', etc.

Links

You may link this activity with: **What's missing? (32)**; **Body movements (54)**; **Classdance (56)**.

Teacher's diary

How did the children do? Did they enjoy the activity? Has the activity taught them a large amount of new language? What other activities can you arrange around the topic 'Shapes'?

---

59 Inventory

Topic	Objects around the classroom
Activity type	Counting
Language	Words related to objects around the classroom; 'there are . . .', 'there is . . .', 'we have . . .'; numbers
Background knowledge	The children should know how to count in the L2 and have a basic knowledge of the words related to the objects that can be seen around the classroom. (It is suggested, therefore, to run this activity after 'Class labels')
Time	25–30 minutes
Classroom setting	Children in groups of 3/5 walking around the classroom
Materials	Pencils, paper
Age	6 and above
Level	Elementary
Purpose	Learning how to count and make simple reports

Preparation

1. Ask the children to take an inventory of things around the classroom. Divide them into small groups. Each group needs pencils and paper to keep records of the results. Encourage the children to count out loud everything they see and make a list of the items that they have counted; for example, desks, chairs, windows, books, maps, blackboards, posters, drawings, calendars, children, plants, etc.

    Have one or two small groups go around the school and make an inventory of the objects they know how to name in the foreign/second language.

2. When the inventories are ready, each group makes a report of the objects that they have listed and compares the results; for example:

> In the classroom there are . . .
> We have . . .

3. The children stick their inventories on the wall.

Links

You may link this activity with: **Who's got the ring? (15)**; **Let's measure up our classroom (60)**; **Class labels (68)**.

Teacher's diary

How did the children do? Was the activity a little bit messy? Did the groups disturb each other? If yes, how could you avoid it? How did the children do when reporting their inventories? Are these kinds of language-learning activities productive? Or do you think there is too much messing around and too little language production after all?

---

60 Let's measure up our classroom

Topic	Measures
Activity type	Making reports
Language	'It's ... long'; 'it's ... high'; 'it's ... wide'
Background knowledge	Numbers
Time	40−50 minutes
Classroom setting	Groups of 3/5
Materials	A large sheet of paper for a wall-chart, tape measures
Age	8 and above
Level	Elementary−intermediate
Purpose	Learning how to measure objects; learning how to make reports about measures

Preparation

Introduce the expressions:

> How long is the ...
> How wide is ...
> How deep ...
> It's 70 cm long.

or perform this activity right after you have come across these expressions in your coursebook.

Ask the children to bring tape measures from home.

In class

1. Write 'Measurements in my classroom' on the wall-chart. Ask the children to tell the names of some objects in the classroom. List these objects on the wall-chart following this format:

	Measurements in my classroom		
	High	Long	Wide
Blackboard			
Door			
Window			
Desks			
Bookcase			
Floor			
Wall			

Divide the children into groups of three to five. Say:

Today we'll measure up our classroom.

Let them go around the classroom measuring up the objects with the tape measure. They note down the appropriate measurements on the wall-chart.

Have one or two groups go outside the classroom to measure the corridor, the plants and other objects around the school.

2. When the children have completed their task, ask them to make a report of the measurements they have taken. They use expressions like:

The desk is 70 centimetres long.

The groups compare the measurements to check if they all got the same.

Links

You may link this activity with: **Inventory (59)**.

Teacher's diary

Did the activity go well? Was it a little bit messy? Did the groups disturb each other? If yes, how could you avoid it? How were the reports done? Do the children think this activity was useful?

---

61 Blind steps

Activity type	Counting
Language	'Take . . .'; 'giant steps', 'baby steps'; 'forward', 'backward', 'left', 'right'
Background knowledge	The children should know how to count in the L2 from 1 to 20
Time	30–40 minutes
Classroom setting	Children standing around the classroom and the playground
Materials	A flag
Age	7 and above
Level	Elementary
Purpose	Learning how to count and give commands

Preparation

Explain the game and its rules given below. Review the words that the children should already know ('left', 'right', 'backward', 'forward'). Introduce the new commands that they need to use; for example, 'take', 'giant steps', 'baby steps', etc.

In class

Divide the children into two teams. The teams stand in the middle of the classroom (or playground) facing each other. Each team needs a player.

Set up a 'starting point'. The two players stand at the 'starting point'. Cover their eyes with a scarf to stop them looking.

Set up an 'arrival' (which can be anywhere in the classroom) and put a flag there. The players — with their eyes covered — have the goal of reaching the arrival and getting the flag. Invite the children in the teams, in turn, to give commands to their players in order to guide them to the flag and get it *first*. The children in each team will help each other in giving the following commands:

> Take five giant steps.
> Take seven baby steps.
> Take three steps forward.
> Take two steps backward.
> Go to the left and take ...
> Go to the right and take ...

Rules:

- The children give one command each time.

- The players count out loud as they take the steps.

- If the players make a mistake while counting they go back to the starting point.

Links

You may link this activity with: **The micro-cities (26)**; **Body movements (54)**; **Classdance (56)**.

Teacher's diary

How did the children do? Was it easy or difficult for them to give the commands?

---

62 Getting ready for 'A day in the life of . . .'

Topic	Characters who belong to children's literature*
Activity type	Learning about foreign cultures
Language	Focus on words (names of characters)
Background knowledge	Literature familiar to children of this age
Time	1 hour
Classroom setting	Any
Materials	Books, magazines, pictures or, if possible, video-tapes of cartoons
Age	7 and above
Level	Elementary and above
Purpose	Getting familiar with popular characters in children's literature

In class

(In L1) Ask the children to tell you the names of popular characters who belong to children's literature. Encourage them to talk about the characters and describe them.

---

*Suggested book characters: Mary Poppins, Pinocchio, Robin Hood, Gulliver, Oliver Twist, Little Red Riding Hood, Sleeping Beauty, Cinderella, Peter Pan, Winnie the Pooh, Popeye, Teddy Ruxpin, the Musketeers, Merlin.

Suggested cartoon characters: Mickey Mouse, Minnie Mouse, Donald Duck, Goofy, Pluto, the Flintstones, Yogi Bear, any others.

1. **(In L2)**   Hand out the books, magazines, pictures that show these characters. Show the video-tapes, if available. Teach the children the characters' names if they do not know them yet.

2. Write down the names on the blackboard to show the correct spelling. Introduce any other interesting character whom they have not mentioned.

3. Ask the children to draw their favourite character — or give them black-and-white drawings of the characters ready made to be coloured. They write the appropriate character's name under the drawing. The children stick their drawings on the wall.

Links

You may link this activity with: **A day in the life of ... (63)**.

Teacher's diary

Did the children find this activity interesting? What characters did they know already? Which were new to them?

---

63 A day in the life of . . .

Topic	Characters who belong to children's literature
Activity type	Playing 'let's pretend'
Language	Words related to the costumes made by the children
Background knowledge	Names of characters
Time	1 full hour dressed up
Classroom setting	Any
Materials	They will be created by the fantasy of the children
Age	7 and above
Level	Elementary and above
Purpose	Getting familiar with popular characters in children's literature; describing the characters

Preparation

See previous activity.

In many elementary schools there is one day of the year dedicated to the 'book'. On that day students, teachers and, at times, the principal dress up as their favourite character in a famous (or less famous) book. This is a pleasant way to inform children about literature and, as a consequence, an encouragement to read books.

Together with the children, decide on an appropriate date for 'A day in the life of . . .'. On that day the children bring appropriate materials (old clothes, paper, various objects) in order to dress up as their favourite character. The children do not need to be 'expensively' dressed up; in fact, the costumes can also be made of paper.

In class

1. Children dress up with your help. Then they go around the class and say:

   > I am Little Red Riding Hood. Who are you?

   or

   > I am Mary Poppins. Are you Pinocchio?

   Give them enough time to show off around the class.

2. Arrange the children in a circle. Teach them some words related to their clothes or to particular features; for example:

   > Little Red Riding Hood: red, basket, apron.

   Ask them to repeat the words after you.
   Each child parades in front of the class.

3. Build up sentences:

   > Little Red Riding Hood carries a basket. She wears a skirt and an apron.

   Do the same with other characters. Then start asking questions:

Teacher	Who has a basket?
Children	Little Red Riding Hood.
Teacher	Who wears a hat?
Children	Mary Poppins.
Teacher	Who has feathers?
Children	Donald Duck.
Teacher	Who has a long nose and is made of wood?
Children	Pinocchio.

   Use gestures while asking questions.

Variations

Make it difficult

Ask the children to think of a character and make a brief description of him or her without mentioning the name. The group has to guess who the character is.

Links

You may link this activity with: **The 'ME' poster (51)**; **Getting ready for 'A day in the life of …' (62)**.

64   Halloween

Topic	Halloween
Activity type	Learning about foreign cultures
Language	Words related to the topic
Time	30−35 minutes
Classroom setting	Any
Materials	A pumpkin with eyes, mouth, nose cut out; a candle; a box or a shopping bag; a set of pictures of Halloween customs cut out from cartoons or books of L2 culture (if available)
Age	6 and above
Level	Elementary and above
Purpose	Informing about Halloween; producing correct L2 sentences

Preparation

1. Get as much information as you can about Halloween (its history, its tradition).

2. During the month of October talk to the children about the tradition of Halloween in the United States and Canada. Tell them that on Halloween day Canadian, American and occasionally British children:

   • Dress up.

   • Talk about ghost stories.

   • Meet at playgrounds or at shopping centres where they play games organised for them by the adults.

- Go around friends' houses or shops saying 'trick or treat'.

  Their friends and shop owners keep a basket ready full of treats to give to the dressed-up children. They are afraid of the 'tricks' that the children might play if they do not get a 'treat'.

  Encourage the children to compare this festivity with the tradition of their own country. Show the pictures of Halloween to give them a visual idea of the customs.

3. Tell the children that on Halloween day you will organise a 'Halloween morning' at school. On that day they will be free to dress up as they want.

4. At home get a pumpkin. Empty it with a knife. Prepare the face by making holes for the eyes, the mouth and the nose, as shown in the picture. Put it in a box together with a candle and matches. You will call it 'Jack o' Lantern'.

   If you cannot find a pumpkin, make a drawing of it or prepare a papier mâché Jack o' Lantern. It is quite easy to cover an inflated balloon with pasted paper strips, then burst the balloon when the paste is hard.

5. Prepare a bag of sweets or little 'treats' (e.g. balloons, coloured pencils, crayons, small toy cars, etc.).

In class

1. On 'Halloween morning' close the shutters of the classroom windows so the children cannot see what you are doing. Create a thrilling atmosphere.

   Put the candle in the pumpkin. Light it up. Take the pumpkin out of the box. The reactions of the children will be prompt. Some will scream, some will laugh, some others will clap hands, etc.

2. Open the shutters and tell the children that they are free to dress up (if they have not done so yet) and go around the classroom asking for 'trick or treat'. The children exchange treats and you give them yours.

3. When all the treats have been given, ask the children to make drawings about Halloween on the blackboard. Expect them to draw a pumpkin, ghosts, witches, masks, sweets, toys or the other objects you have given them. Teach them the appropriate words for each drawing.

Variations

Expand

Keep your treats and all the treats collected among the children. Ask them to produce correct sentences in the L2, preferably about Halloween. If the sentence is correct, say 'TREAT!' and throw the treat to the child who said it. If the sentence is wrong, say 'TRICK, sorry, try again!' and do not throw any treats. Go ahead until you have finished all the treats and the children have produced lots of sentences.

Make it difficult

The children walk into other L2 classes. They ask their peers for tricks or treats. If the children want to they can do the following:

- Play a short funny sketch in front of the new group.

- Make a short report on the Halloween tradition.

Links

You may link this activity with: **A birthday gift (41)**.

Teacher's diary

Was it difficult to organise this activity? Did the children enjoy it? Did they show interest in the information you gave them? How much new language did they learn? What other language-learning activities can be built up like this one?

SECTION IV

TIME FOR READING

65 Picture compound words

Topic	Compound words
Activity type	Playing with words
Language	Focus on words related to the topic
Background knowledge	The children should have some basic vocabulary knowledge
Time	25–30 minutes
Classroom setting	Any
Materials	A set of cards
Age	7 and above
Level	Elementary–intermediate
Purpose	Learning and reviewing compound words and making learners aware of how compounds are formed

Preparation

Photocopy* the words provided for you on page 165. Cut them out and stick them on cards. Draw or cut out pictures from magazines of the following items:

a book of fairy-tales	a fireman
an airplane	a birthday cake
a sailboat	a football
a toy truck	a skateboard
a doghouse	a playground
a boyscout	a toothbrush

*You are permitted to photocopy these pages for classroom use.

a snowman   a schoolbus
a classroom   a crossword

A set of cards is now ready to be used by the children in class. If possible, prepare more than one set. You can have four or five similar sets for group work. You can also prepare different sets if you are willing to add other compounds and other pictures made by you to the ones suggested here.

In class

Divide the children into teams of four or five. Give them the cards. Tell them they have to do the following:

- Make up the compounds.

- Match them to the appropriate pictures.

Help them when they find difficulties with unfamiliar words.
    At the end, groups compare what they have put down and compounds are read aloud.

Variations

Make it difficult

Ask the children to make up sentences with the compounds.

Links

You may link this activity with: **Compound words (66)**; **Words in sight (67)**.

Teacher's diary

How did the children do? Did they enjoy matching the compounds with the pictures? Could they do it easily? Was it difficult for you to prepare the sets of cards? If yes, how can you make it simpler? What other compounds would you introduce in the same way?

fairy	plane	sail	class
house	boy	man	air
truck	tales	boat	ground
snow	play	fire	ball
birth	day	room	scout
toy	tooth	brush	school
foot	dog	board	man
bus	cross	skate	word

66 Compound words

Topic	Compound words
Activity type	Playing with words
Language	Focus on words related to the topic
Background knowledge	The children should have been previously exposed to the words they find in the activity
Time	25–30 minutes
Classroom setting	Any
Materials	A set of cards
Age	8 and above
Level	Intermediate
Purpose	Learning and reviewing compound words and making learners aware of how compounds are formed

Preparation

As in the previous activity, photocopy* the words provided for you on page 167. Cut them out and stick them on cards. A set of cards is now ready to be used by the children in class.

In class

The procedure is similar to the one suggested in the previous activity. The children have to match the words to make up appropriate compounds. When the children have completed their matching, ask them to make up drawings for each compound.

*You are permitted to photocopy these pages for classroom use.

Here the children do not have any visual aid and this, consequently, makes the activity more difficult. You will probably need to give them more assistance.

Play these two activities on compounds several times during a term until the children have become self-confident in recognising the compound words. Add two or three new compounds every time you play the game again.

Variations

Make it difficult

Ask the children to make up sentences with the compounds.

Links

You may link this activity with: **Picture compound words (65)**; **Words in sight (67)**.

Teacher's diary

Was this activity more difficult than the 'Picture compound words' (65)? How did the children do this time? How many compounds could they match? What other compounds would you introduce in the same way?

---

every	home	base	farm
box	walkie	day	straw
noon	ball	after	sun
talkie	mail	board	house
surf	ice	work	berry
black	cream	wind	set

67   Words in sight

Topic	Topic related words
Activity type	Learning and recognising words
Language	Focus on words related to the topic
Background knowledge	The children should have been previously exposed to the words they come across in the activity
Time	20–40 minutes
Classroom setting	Children playing in groups of 3/4
Materials	Photocopy of the visual aids provided for you here; a set of small flashcards; some clips
Age	7 and above
Level	Elementary–intermediate
Purpose	Learning and reviewing words and making learners aware of their meaning

Preparation

1. Make circular composite drawings (the number depends on how many groups you want to have in class) similar to those shown on page 169. Stick them on circular pieces of cardboard.

2. Write the names of the objects on the back of each picture.

3. Prepare a set of flashcards and write the names of the objects on them, as shown on page 169.

In class

1.   Divide the children into groups of 3 or 4. Give each group a circular board, its set of cards and some clips. They have to clip the words to the appropriate pictures.

2.   When they are ready, the groups compare what the others have done and read the words aloud to each other. If there are disagreements they check the appropriate answer by looking at the words printed on the back.

Variations

Make it difficult

Add more words to the ones provided here. Prepare the cardboards with the new pictures and the set of flashcards with the new words. This time the sets will all be different from each other. Each group plays, therefore, with different words. When the groups have completed their clipping and checking, they exchange their cardboards with the others until all the cardboards have been passed through the groups (obviously, each group 'unclips' the 'word cards' before passing the board to the others).

Links

You may link this activity with: **Picture compound words (65)**; **Compound words (66)**.

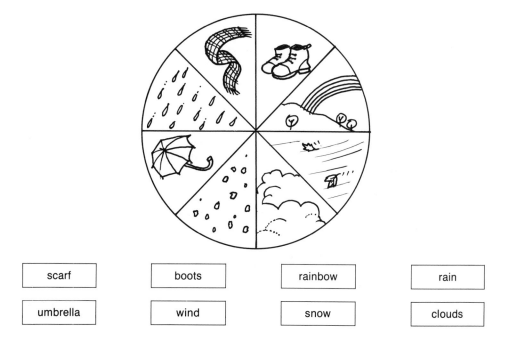

| scarf | boots | rainbow | rain |
| umbrella | wind | snow | clouds |

68 Class labels

Topic	Classroom objects
Activity type	Learning and recognising words
Language	Focus on words related to the topic
Time	30–35 minutes
Classroom setting	Any
Materials	A set of rectangular cards
Age	6 and above
Level	Beginners and above
Purpose	Learning how to name classroom objects; learning the appropriate spelling of the words; early introduction to reading skills

In class

1. Tell the children to look around the classroom and observe the objects in it. Teach them the words for these objects in the L2. Let them repeat after you while pointing at the objects.

2. Write the words on the blackboard at random. Do it while eliciting them from the children. Point at a word and ask a child to read it. Go on until all of them can recognise the words easily.

3. Give the set of cards to a group of children. They write the names of the objects on them by copying the words from the blackboard. Meanwhile, another group of children sticks the labels around the classroom in the appropriate place.

    Do not 'crowd' the children's minds with too many words at a time. Perform this activity two or three times until the room is covered with 'word' labels all around.

Label also the unthought-of objects; for example, floor, ceiling, spider's web (if available!), etc. This is also a way to 'personalise' the look of your classroom and get the children busy decorating it.

Variations

Expand

Revise the words from time to time by doing the following:

- Asking the children to read them.

- Taking the labels off and asking the children to name the objects.

Links

You may link this activity with: **Extra cards? Put them in the pocket (44)**; **Inventory (59)**.

Teacher's diary

What does the classroom look like now? Are the children proud of their labels? Do they ask to add others? Do they use the labels as vocabulary references? Do you think the labels help them remember the words and their spelling?

---

69 Choose what to say

Topic	Everyday situations
Activity type	Using everyday expressions
Language	Formulaic expressions
Background knowledge	Basic knowledge of the formulaic expressions used in the activity
Time	20 minutes
Classroom setting	Children standing around the classroom
Materials	Two sets of cards, each set in a different colour
Age	8 and above
Level	Intermediate
Purpose	Becoming aware of the accurate use of everyday expressions

Preparation

Prepare two sets of cards with expressions already familiar to the children. One is the set of 'Situations'. Write this set in the children's L1 to facilitate the task. The other is the set of 'Expressions' (see some examples below).

In class

1. Divide the children into two large groups. Give the set of cards related to 'Situations' to a group and the set of cards related to 'Expressions' to the other group. Each child will have one single card. Tell them to read the card they have.

2. Tell them to look for a partner* in the other group so they can match the 'Situation' and 'Expression' cards; for example:

> You meet a friend   Hi!
> (use L1)

When the children have found their partners, the matching cards are read aloud for group checking.

Situations	Expressions	
You meet a friend	I'm sorry	So sorry
You have done something wrong	Thank you very much	Thanks
It's time to go home	Yippee!	Hi!
You meet your teacher	I'll see you tomorrow	Good morning
You are having a wonderful time	This is not fair	How are you doing?
Somebody has done something wrong to you	This is fun!	Yummy!
You are buying an ice-cream	Yuk!	
You don't like what you are eating		

Variations

Make it difficult

Give the 'Situations' in English.

Links

You may link this activity with: **Rush the sentence (4)**; **Bubbles search (75)**.

Teacher's diary

How did the children do? Was it difficult to find their partners? Did any of them look lost while doing the activity? Did they help each other? Did you let them help each other?

---

*Or partners, since one situation can have more than one appropriate expression; e.g. 'I'm sorry', 'So sorry!'

70 The 'what, when, where, how' game

Topic	Any
Activity type	Building up sentences
Language	Varied
Background knowledge	The children should have achieved basic skills in reading and sentence formation. They should be familiar with 'WH' expressions
Time	45−50 minutes
Classroom setting	Children working in groups of 3/5
Materials	Four sets of cards, each set in a different colour; a large piece of paper
Age	8 and above
Level	Elementary and above
Purpose	Practising sentence formation; accuracy and cohesiveness

Preparation

Prepare four sets of cards in four different colours. Each colour represents one of the following four groups of phrases, for example:

the 'What' phrases → yellow
the 'When' phrases → pink
the 'Where' phrases → light blue
the 'How' phrases → green

Copy the phrases provided for you in the list below on the appropriate coloured cards.

Add more phrases (or change them) according to the competence of your group of children.

When		What	
In the morning	After lunch	I go	I watch cartoons
After school	At the week-ends	Boys and girls ride mountain bikes	Children play
At night	On Sunday morning	Babies cry	I stay

Where		How	
in their beds	in the playground	noisily	happily
on TV	to school	calmly	heavily
in bed	on bad roads	carefully	lazily

Get a large piece of paper. Write the headings 'What', 'When', 'Where', 'How' on top of it. Make sure you leave some space from one heading to another.

In class

1. Divide the children into four groups. Give each group one set of cards as in the layout in the illustration.

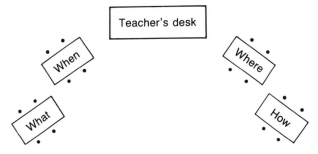

2. The 'When' group reads the first phrase. In turn, and following cohesive sentence building, the other groups check their cards and add the appropriate linking phrase, for example:

> | In the morning | | I go | | to school | | lazily |

3. Get the piece of paper. When a full correct sentence is completed, the children dictate it to you. You will transcribe it on the paper for future reading.

4. Stick the poster on the wall.

Links

You may link this activity with: **Jigsaw story (71)**.

71   Jigsaw story

Topic	Stories
Activity type	Reading for pleasure
Language	The language focus will come out of the story or stories that you have selected
Background knowledge	Basic reading skills
Time	40–60 minutes
Classroom setting	Any
Materials	Photocopies from books
Age	9 and above
Level	Intermediate and above
Purpose	Improving understanding of the sequence of events presented in a text

Preparation

Select a picture story or cartoon suitable to the L2 reading ability of the children. It must follow an obvious sequence of events. Photocopy it. Cut up the story to have sets of sentences, and mix it up. Stick the cut-out pieces on cards.* Or put the pieces together again but in jumbled order. Make new photocopies of the jumbled up story.

In class

1.   Divide the children into groups of three to five. Give each group the story. Tell

*Have as many sets as the number of groups you want to have in class.

them to rebuild the story in the appropriate order. Go around to give help. Encourage discussion about the story even if the discussion is in the children's L1.

2.   The groups compare in what order they have rebuilt the story.

3.   Ask each group questions to provoke a short report about the story that they have 'reordered'. Can each group say the following:

- The title of the story.

- The names of the main characters.

- The words and expressions they read and recognised.

- What the story is about in broad outline.

- How many pictures they found.

- What these pictures show.

- Whether the story looked long or short to them.

Add any other points you think are relevant to 'talk' about the story. Ask these questions in the children's L1, if necessary.

Variations

Make it difficult

Ask advanced students to make a report about the story.

Expand

Ask advanced students to take the role of the characters of the story and make up a dialogue based on a sketch of the story.

Links

You may link this activity with: **The 'what, when, where, how' game (70)**; **Your story, my writing (78)**; and with **First day at school (22)**; **Play shop (23)**; **Going to the doctor (24)**.

Teacher's diary

How well did the children do? Did they use their L1 while doing the activity? Did they have difficulties doing the task? If yes, what kind of difficulties were they? How much of the passage did they actually understand: general information or details?

---

72 Read 'n' shout

Topic	Any
Activity type	Reading aloud
Language	Focus on pronunciation
Background knowledge	Basic reading skills
Time	20–25 minutes
Classroom setting	Any
Materials	A reading passage on a topic familiar to the children
Age	8 and above
Level	Elementary and above, depending on the difficulty of the passage
Purpose	Practising correct pronunciation of words; producing intonation appropriate to the meaning of the passage

Preparation

Select a short passage suitable to the children's level of reading proficiency in the L2. Use a story the children have read before or know well.

In class

1. Give the passage to the children. Ask them to read it silently. Ask a few general comprehension questions (L1 accepted). Read yourself with some exaggerated 'mistakes' to demonstrate the activity, and show that mistakes are made by everyone.

2. Ask a child to start reading the passage aloud. When she makes a pronunciation mistake her fellow students 'shout' the correction of the mispronounced word at her. This must be done in a kind, light-hearted way. The teacher then appoints a student to take over and continue reading until she is interrupted by the others.

This goes on until the text is read in a way 'accepted' by the class.

Links

You may link this activity with: **The 'How do you read it?' game (73).**

Teacher's diary

To what extent has this activity helped the children pronounce words and phrases correctly? Has the repetitive reading helped them improve? Did they enjoy 'shouting' the words? How did the reader react?

---

73 The 'How do you read it?' game

Topic	Stories
Activity type	Reading aloud
Language	Related to the story introduced
Background knowledge	The children should have good reading skills
Time	40–45 minutes
Classroom setting	Any
Materials	A reading passage on a topic familiar to the children; a set of flashcards
Age	8 and above
Level	Intermediate and advanced
Purpose	Reading aloud using drama techniques

Preparation

1. Select a passage appropriate to your learners' reading ability in the L2.

2. Prepare a set of cards to be given to the children. On each card write the 'role' in which you want the children to read the story or passage, for example:

    Read the story as if:

    - You were a speaker on the television.

    - You were angry with everybody else in the world.

    - You were a mother reading a bedtime story to your child.

- It were a happy story.

- It were a sad story.

- It were the most boring story ever read.

Write the cards in the children's L1.

In class

1. Give the passage to the children. Ask them to read it silently and focus on the meaning. Give them the chance to ask you any questions about unfamiliar words or meanings — although there should not be too many if your selection of a passage is accurate. Ask them questions to check they have full comprehension of the story.

2. Divide them into large groups of 'readers' and 'listeners'. Give the cards to the 'readers' (one per child). Let them read your instructions and rehearse for a few minutes.

3. Meanwhile, write the 'roles' that the 'readers' will cover on the blackboard (in L1). This will function as a guide for the 'listeners'.

4. The reading session starts. The 'listeners' listen to their peers' reading aloud and, at the end, say in what 'role' each child has performed.

Links

You may link this activity with: **Read 'n' shout (72)**; **The 'What do you read?' game (74)**.

Teacher's diary

How well did the children do? Were some 'reader' roles difficult for them? If yes, what other roles could you think of? How well did the 'listeners' do?

---

74 The 'What do you read?' game

Topic	Letters, messages, short notes
Activity type	Reading aloud
Language	Related to the topics
Background knowledge	The children should have good reading skills
Time	30−40 minutes
Classroom setting	Any
Materials	A set of reading passages on topics familiar to the children
Age	9 and above
Level	Intermediate and advanced, depending on the difficulty of the passage
Purpose	Practising reading aloud to other people

Preparation

1. Select (or make up) a set of four or five reading passages appropriate to your learners' reading ability in the L2. The passages may be one of the following:

    A message to be read to a friend on the telephone.
    The homework noted on the blackboard to be read to a friend who has lost his glasses.
    A letter from a penfriend.
    A postcard from a friend on holiday.
    A set of instructions for a new tape-recorder or computer.
    A set of instructions on a box of video-games.
    A set of instructions for a recipe.

Information about sports games written on the bulletin board.
A short scientific passage about animals threatened with extinction (or any other topics).

Choose any others appropriate to the children's age and interests.

In class

1. Select a group of four or five children who have good reading skills. Give each of them a passage. Tell them that they have to read it to their classmates. Let them rehearse for a short while if they want to.

2. Write a list of what kind of passages the children will be listening to on the blackboard. (See the examples above.)

3. Tell the class that they are going to listen to their classmates reading to them. Their task is to understand *what* they are reading. They do it by selecting the appropriate answer from the list that you have provided for them on the blackboard.

Links

You may link this activity with: **The 'How do you read it?' game (73).**

Teacher's diary

How did the children like the activity? Were the passages difficult for them? Was it difficult for you to search for short passages of the kinds suggested in the activity? What other passages would you select for your students? Was the class motivated enough to listen?

---

75 Bubbles search

Topic	Any
Activity type	Reading for pleasure
Language	Based on the topics that you choose
Background knowledge	Basic experience in reading skills
Time	20−30 minutes
Classroom setting	Any
Materials	Cut-out pictures of activities; home-prepared 'speech bubbles'
Age	8 and above
Level	From elementary to advanced, depending on the difficulty of the 'speech bubble' captions
Purpose	Reinforcing reading comprehension

Preparation

Prepare cut-out or draw pictures showing an activity or situation containing people. Cartoons with animals speaking are popular. Prepare suitable 'speech bubbles' to indicate what the people might be saying; for example:

Picture	Speech bubble
Child eating an ice-cream	I love ice-cream!
Child surrounded by books	It's hard to read all these books!
Child surrounded by lots of things falling out of a cupboard	What a mess!
Man hitting his hand with a hammer	Ouch!
Boy playing soccer	Soccer is my favourite sport.

In class

1. Divide the children into groups of three to five. Give them the pictures and the speech bubbles. Ask them to look at the pictures, read the content of the bubbles and do the appropriate matching.

2. The groups compare what matching they have done.

   Use this activity more than once during a term. Every time change pictures and bubbles.

Variations

Expand and integrate with writing

Leave some speech bubbles without captions. Ask the children to write appropriate expressions in them.

Links

You may link this activity with: **Choose what to say (69).**

Teacher's diary

Were the children able to do the matching? Would you repeat this activity with different pictures and captions? Where can you find pictures and speech bubbles of this kind?

---

76 If walls talk you read them

Topic	Varied
Activity type	Reading for pleasure
Language	Related to the topic
Background knowledge	Basic experience in reading skills
Time	30–40 minutes
Classroom setting	Any
Materials	Papers, pencils
Age	All ages
Level	Elementary and above, depending on what is displayed on the walls and how much language the posters contain
Purpose	Reviewing past activities; reflecting on past activities; evaluating the work done so far

Preparation

Find any possible opportunities to prepare a poster, a set of drawings or any visual thing to be done together with the children. Display these visuals as often as you can.

When the walls are full up with 'things to say', and approximately once a month, organise a 'walking around' reading session.

In class

1. Tell the children to walk around the room with a piece of paper and a pencil, look at the posters and note down the following:

- Words that they like.

- Words/expressions they remember well.

- Words/expressions they do not remember.

- Spelling mistakes.

- Any other you can think of.

Write these points on the blackboard to facilitate their task. Ask them to use headings on their papers under which they can list their notes. Choose only one or two points with younger children.

2. At the end, each of the children makes a simple, brief report on the posters (L1 admitted).

3. Ask the children to select the poster (or posters) they have enjoyed looking at best. This can become 'The poster of the month'.

Links

This activity can be linked with a large number of activities previously presented. Many of them, in fact, require the preparation of posters and consequently lead to this activity.

Teacher's diary

How long did it take to have the classroom covered with posters? Was it useful for the children to look back at all of them? How much language was familiar to them? What did they not remember? Did they find any mistakes?

---

77 Book 'n' balloons

Topic	Content of books
Activity type	Reading for pleasure
Language	Focus on reading skill
Background knowledge	The children should have developed good reading skills
Time	From one hour to one week
Materials	Elementary readers
Age	8 and above
Level	Elementary and above, depending on the difficulty of the readers
Purpose	Encouraging extensive reading; focusing on general information about a book

Preparation

Bring to class a set of elementary-level readers for your students. Keep it in the classroom in your English corner.

In class

Show the books around and help the children become familiar with the most relevant features of the books (e.g. title, author, pictures, content, etc.). Encourage them 'to look at the books' during a reading session that you may frequently schedule or invite them to borrow the books for 'home reading'. Tell the children that they *do not need* to understand all the details in the book. Their easy task is, instead, to fill in the book report shown below in the format of a set of balloons.

    Every time a set of balloons has been filled in, the child colours it, cuts it out and hangs it on the wall, in the 'reading corner'.

Variations

Change the format of the book report from time to time; for example, a butterfly, a tree, an apple, a flower, a kite, etc.

Links

You may link this activity with: **Shall we read a fairy-tale? (81)**.

Teacher's diary

Are the children interested in extensive reading? Do they feel challenged by activities of this kind? Or do they think that the task is too hard for them? How many ask to read books? How many are willing to complete the balloons? How often do they do it? What can you do for the ones who find this activity difficult?

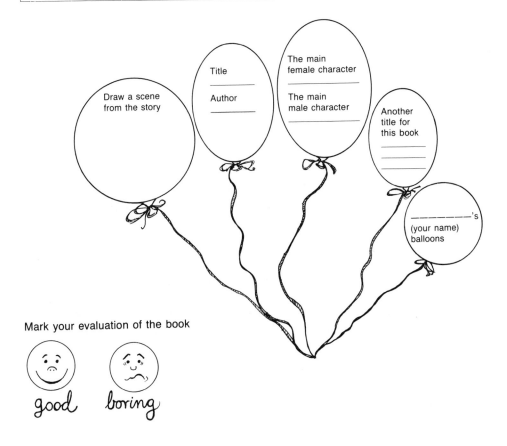

78 Your story, my writing

Topic	Any chosen by the children
Activity type	Reading for pleasure
Language	The language focus will come out of the stories told by the children
Background knowledge	Basic reading skills
Time	Two different sessions of 50−60 minutes
Classroom setting	Any
Materials	Papers, pencils, crayons
Age	8 and above
Level	Intermediate and advanced
Purpose	Creating L2 texts starting from L1 children's stories; motivating children to read in the L2; encouraging L2 reading skills

In class

1. **(In L1)** Tell the children that they are going to tell a story in their L1. Give a simple beginning of a story. Ask the children, in turn, to continue the story and find an appropriate ending. Take note of all the expressions they use.

    When their story is finished, show the children that you have understood their story by retelling it. Be cohesive and concise while you do it.

2. **(Art)** Give the children papers, pencils and crayons. Tell them that now they will retell the same story through drawings. Each of them (or in pairs) chooses to draw a different scene from the story. Collect the drawings.

Preparation

Rewrite the children's story in the L2 by describing the drawings produced. Copy it onto the drawings. Match the expressions with the scenes described in the drawings. There should be one or two sentences per drawing.

In class

1. **(In L2)** Display the papers (with drawings and story) at random. Ask the children to put the papers in order (the drawings will help). Read the story — ready-made in the L2 — to the children. Help them to read it aloud after you. How do they like it now?

2. Focus on the text by following these steps:

   • Ask easy comprehension questions.

   • Focus on new relevant words.

   • Focus on a specific point of grammar that occurs in the story and that the children are not familiar with; for example, simple present, simple past, future tense, etc.

3. The children stick their drawings with the story on the wall.

Variations

Make it difficult

Write the expressions describing the story on separate flashcards. Ask the children to read the flashcards, put them in order and match them to the appropriate pictures.

Links

You may link this activity with: **Jigsaw story (71)**.

Teacher's diary

Did all the children give their little contribution to the story? How much new language have the children learned? If the activity worked well would you repeat it? If it did not work as expected how would you improve it? To what extent can this activity contribute to the development of reading and writing skills?

79 A noisy story, a noisy picture

Topic	A simple 'noisy' story
Activity type	Listening to a story
Language	Verbs that express noisy actions
Background knowledge	Basic listening skills
Time	40–50 minutes
Classroom setting	Any
Materials	A short story to be read to the children
Age	7 and above
Level	Elementary and above, depending on how difficult the story is
Purpose	Improving understanding of a text read by the teacher

Preparation

Write a short passage using verbs that express noisy actions. An example is given here:

Sometimes it feels good to be noisy in class. When I read a story to you I can hear lots of little and big noises going around. I am right at the beginning of the story and ... Maria *claps* her hands, Sonia *sings*, Martina *dances* on her chair and Sara *roars*.

I keep on reading the story when ... Johnny and Mario *stamp* their feet, Franco and Alex *giggle*, Anna and Emma *shout*, Betty and Nancy *cheer*.

I get to the end of the story and ... Danny and Emily *laugh*, Benny and Michi *scream*, Laura and Flo *yell*. How hard it is to read a story to a gang of noisy children like you!

In class

1. Read the story to the children. When you mention a 'noisy' verb for the first time, make the appropriate gestures or actions to help the children understand the meaning of it. Following your example, and when they hear their names, they perform the 'noisy' actions. They keep on doing the noises until the end of the story. Therefore, there will be an increasing crescendo of noises around the classroom. Do it a few times until the children are getting familiar with their 'noisy' verbs. Then start making different matchings of names and verbs to allow the children to make different noises and get familiar with the whole set of verbs that you have mentioned in the story.

2. Elicit the 'noisy' verbs from the children and write them on the blackboard. Help the children read them.

3. Ask the children to make a 'noisy' drawing in which they describe what is happening in the story. They write down the 'noisy' verbs next to the drawings that describe them.

Variations

Make it difficult

Ask the children to write a short paragraph describing their drawings.

Links

You may link this activity with: **A quiet story, a quiet picture (80)**.

Teacher's diary

Did the children enjoy the activity? How much new language have they learned?

---

80   A quiet story, a quiet picture

Topic	A simple 'quiet' story
Activity type	Listening to a story
Language	Adjectives that express a quiet atmosphere
Background knowledge	Basic listening skills
Time	40–50 minutes
Classroom setting	Any
Materials	A short story to be read to the children
Age	7 and above
Level	Elementary and above, depending on how difficult the story is
Purpose	Improving understanding of a text read by the teacher

Preparation

Write a short passage using adjectives that express a quiet atmosphere. An example is given to you here.

> It's a rainy day. Sonia is at home. She looks through the window. Everything is so *quiet* outside and at home there is such a *peaceful* atmosphere. She looks around the room. Everything is so *cosy*, the fire is burning in the fireplace and Sonia feels *warm*. The cat is sleeping near the fire, he looks so *soft* and *snug* under his *fluffy* blanket. Sonia is *happy*.

In class

1. Write the set of 'quiet' adjectives on the blackboard. Explain the meaning, if necessary. Help the children pronounce them appropriately.

2. Read the story to the children. When you mention a 'quiet' adjective, the children have to put their hands up to show that they have recognised it and repeat it aloud. Do it a few times until the children become familiar with these new 'quiet' adjectives.

3. Check if the children have understood the meaning of the story. If not, give some help.

4. Ask the children to make a 'quiet' picture in which they describe what is happening in the story. They write down the 'quiet' adjectives next to the drawings that describe them.

Variations

Make it difficult

Ask the children to write a short paragraph describing their drawings.

Links

You may link this activity with: **A noisy story, a noisy picture (79)**.

Teacher's diary

Did the children enjoy this activity? How much new language have they learned? What other 'themes' can you think of for activities like this one or the previous one? How about 'A sunny story, a sunny picture'? Can you think of any others?

81   Shall we read a fairy-tale?

Topic	Fairy-tales
Activity type	Listening to a story
Language	The language focus will come out of the story you have chosen
Background knowledge	Basic skills in understanding written texts
Time	40–45 minutes
Classroom setting	Any, but preferably children sitting in a circle on the floor around the teacher
Materials	Elementary books of short stories; papers, pencils, crayons
Age	7–11
Level	Elementary and above, depending on how difficult the story is
Purpose	Improving understanding of a text read by the teacher

Preparation

Select an easy-to-follow story from the school library, if available, or your own library. Choose a topic that children enjoy. Make sure that the story is illustrated with lively pictures.

In class

1. **(In L1)**   Invite the children to sit around you in a relaxed, cosy atmosphere. Show the pictures and ask what they think the story is about. Elicit their ideas, then introduce the story.

2. **(In L2)**   Tell them:

> Now you are going to listen to this story in English.

Read the story aloud while pointing at the pictures. Look around at your students' eyes trying to catch their attention. Be careful about pauses, stress and gestures that may accompany the story. They may understand very little but may be attracted by the sounds of your voice and the movements you make.
> When you finish, be silent for a few moments; wait for the children's reactions.

3. Ask — in the L1 — what they have understood of the story, what names they remember, what words sounded familiar to them.

4. Ask the children to get paper and crayons and say:

> Now think about the story and make a drawing of it.

Go around the desks and ask about what they are drawing (L1 admitted). Make comments (in L2: 'Very good'; 'I like it'; 'Interesting'; 'Funny!').
> Invite them to write a few L2 words or expressions that may describe their drawings.

5. Stick the drawings on the wall. The children write the title of the story in big letters and put it on top of their drawings.

Variations

Make it difficult

Ask the children to write a short paragraph describing their drawings.

Links

You may link this activity with: **Book 'n' balloons (77)**.

Teacher's diary

Did the children like the activity? Would they like to listen to you reading to them again? How can you select suitable motivating stories? To what extent can this activity and the whole 'reading for pleasure' section develop the children's reading ability and their motivation to read?

SECTION V

TIME FOR WRITING

82 Show me your folder

Topic	Varied
Activity type	Writing
Language	The language focus is related to the writing activities performed by the children
Classroom setting	Any
Materials	Rewards photocopied from this book (see 'Time for rewards', section VI); 'reward' stickers (if available); 'reward' rubber stamps (if available)
Age	6 and above
Level	Elementary and above
Purpose	Encouraging children to become aware of the activities they have carried out and of their own progress; checking writing activities performed by the children

Preparation

From the first days of L2 instruction tell the children to bring a 'folder' to class. Encourage them to use their folders when you realise that they are interested in seeing how a word or a short expression is written. Do not be afraid of introducing written forms of words too early, since reading and writing need not follow oral development but may be parallel to it and contribute to general language control.

Let the students copy the words and make drawings next to them to show the appropriate meaning. At the end of every month or when you think it is appropriate, tell the children that there will be a 'folder day'.

In class

1. On 'folder day' invite the children to look at each other's folders and make comments.

2. Tell them to choose the pages that they like best and tell you the reasons. Suggest they think of reasons, such as the following:

    > It was a nice activity.
    > They just like their own drawings.
    > They like the words noted down on that page.
    > They like the organisation of the page.
    > They like it because it is a messy page.

    Or any other reasons that you think appropriate for them.

3. While their comments and descriptions are going on, go around the classroom, look at the folders and put rewards on their pages using drawings photocopied from 'Time for rewards', stickers, rubber stamps or just your marker. Obviously, comments and descriptions will be in the children's mother tongue. This does not really matter since L2 themes and L2 activities previously carried out will be the topics of their discussions. This will increase their awareness of what has been done in classes so far.

Links

You may link this activity with: **Time for rewards (section VI)**.

Teacher's diary

Does this activity encourage the children to look back at their schoolwork? Is this useful for them? Do they often expect rewards? Do you give them enough and appropriate rewards?

---

83   Runaway capitals

Topic	Varied
Activity type	Writing
Language	Focus on capital letters
Background knowledge	The children should have basic skills in reading and writing
Time	25–30 minutes
Classroom setting	Any
Materials	A written story selected from the children's coursebook or any other source; a wall-chart; a set of small cards
Age	8 and above
Level	Elementary and intermediate, depending on content of story
Purpose	Increasing the children's ability to use capital letters appropriately

Preparation

Select a story suitable for the children's knowledge of the L2. Use the coursebook (if available) or any other books as your source. Write the story without using capital letters (leave punctuation, though) in large letters on a wall-chart, for example:

'tom', 'i', 'april', 'may', 'christmas', 'santa claus', 'new york', 'sue', plus all the letters at the beginning of sentences.

Make sure that there are a few 'I's' which are not at the beginning of sentences in your passage. Many children, in fact, need to reinforce their knowledge of a correct writing of the pronoun 'I'.

Prepare a set of small cards. Write the missing capital letters on the card (one card — one letter).

In class

1. Put the wall-chart on the wall and the capital-letters cards on the table. Ask the children to read the story and replace the inappropriate small letters by sticking the appropriate capital letter cards on them.

2. Ask one child to read the passage aloud to the class. While reading he stresses the words beginning with the capital letter.

3. Check comprehension of the story.

Variations

Make it difficult

Ask the children to copy the story. They will insert the appropriate capital letters.

Links

You may link this activity with: **Choose the punctuation (84)**.

Teacher's diary

Did the children enjoy this easy activity? Does the activity help them become aware of differences (if there are any) in using capital letters between L1 and L2?

---

84 Choose the punctuation

Topic Varied

Activity type Writing

Language Focus on punctuation

Background knowledge The children should have good skills in reading and writing

Time 25–30 minutes

Classroom setting Any

Materials A written story selected from the children's coursebook or any other source; a wall-chart; small round cards

Age 8 and above

Level Elementary and above, depending on content of story

Purpose Increasing the children's ability to be aware of sentence and paragraph formation

Preparation

Select a story suitable to the children's knowledge of the L2. Use the children's coursebook (if available) or any other books as your source. Write the story without using punctuation (but leave capital letters) in large letters on a wall-chart. Prepare small round cards. Write a punctuation symbol on each card, for example:

In class

1. Put the wall-chart on the wall and the punctuation cards on the table. Ask the children to read the story and put the punctuation cards in the appropriate places.

2.   Ask one child to read the passage aloud to the class. While reading he uses gestures and pauses to stress the appropriate punctuation; for example, short pauses for commas, longer pauses for full stops.

3.   Check comprehension of the story.

Variations

Make it difficult

Ask the children to copy the story. They will insert the appropriate punctuation.

Links

You may link this activity with: **Runaway capitals (83)**.

Teacher's diary

Did the children do well? Can this activity help them become aware of sentence and paragraph formation? Are they already aware of it in their L1? Will you use this activity more than once?

85   Make a poem

Topic	Authentic rhymes
Activity type	Writing
Language	Focus on rhyming
Background knowledge	The children should have basic skills in reading
Time	25−30 minutes
Classroom setting	Any
Materials	A rhyme selected from common children's literature; a large sheet of white paper; a few coloured (red) rectangular cards
Age	7 and above (11−14 for the example in the Variations)
Level	Elementary and above, depending on content of poem
Purpose	Increasing the children's ability to recognise rhyming words

Preparation

Choose a rhyme popular among children in the L2 country (or countries). Write it in large letters on the sheet of paper. Leave gaps for the final rhyming words. Draw short lines to show the gaps.

Write the rhyming words on the cards. An example is given below.

Little Jack _____
Sat in the _____,
Eating a Christmas _____;
He put in his _____,

And pulled out a _____,
And said, 'What a good boy am _____!'

| corner | thumb | I | plum | Horner | pie |

In class

1. Show the poster with the rhyme to the children. Read it to them. Ask them if they can think of the missing words. If they guess a right word show the card and stick it on the appropriate place.

    If the children do not guess any words, stick all the cards at random on the blackboard. Read the words to them and make them choose on what line each word goes. Stick on the cards following their suggestions until the rhyme has been completed.

2. Help the children read the rhyme aloud following the appropriate intonation. Explain new vocabulary while this goes on.

3. Encourage the children to retell the rhyme making appropriate gestures linked to the meaning of the rhyme; for example:

    Little Jack Horner
          (they make the gesture of 'little')
    Sat in the corner
          (point at a corner)
    Eating a Christmas pie
          (pretend they are eating)
    He put in his thumb
          (put thumb in an imaginary cake)
    And pulled out a plum
          (pull out an imaginary plum and put it close to mouth)
    And said, 'What a good boy am I!'
          (open hands — palms up — around a smiling face)

4. Ask the children to draw a picture telling about the poem.

Variations

Expand

You can find other rhymes suitable for this activity in any children's books of songs and nursery rhymes. (Some examples are given below.)

Wee Willie Winkie
Runs through the town,
Upstairs and downstairs
In his nightgown.

Humpty Dumpty sat on a wall,
Humpty Dumpty had a great fall,
All the king's horses and all the king's men
Couldn't put Humpty together again.

'Baa baa black sheep
Have you any wool?'
'Yes sir, yes sir,
Three bags full.
One for the master,
One for the dame
And one for the little girl
Who lives down the lane.'

Make it difficult

Encourage older learners to make up their own poems. You can do it as a follow-up
to an activity in which you have presented a poem or a song.

Links

You may link this activity with: **Ring-a-ring-a-rosy (8)**.

Teacher's diary

If you have used the activity with grown-up students as suggested in the
variations, how many students have come up with their own poems? Did
they need your help or were they autonomous? How can you encourage
them to write more poems?

---

86 Your 'closest' pen-friend

Topic	Letters
Activity type	Writing
Language	Varied
Background knowledge	The children should have basic skills in reading and writing
Time	30−50 minutes
Classroom setting	Any
Materials	Paper for letters and envelopes
Age	9 and above
Level	Intermediate and above
Purpose	Increasing the children's ability to communicate in letters and messages

Preparation

There will be one day on which the children ask you how to write a message to a friend, a card or a short letter to a relative living far away. At that point tell them that they can write to a friend regularly if they wish to.

Choose another class where you (or another active teacher like you) teach the L2. Tell the children in this new class that they will soon receive some mail from friends.

Tell the children in your class that there will be a 'mail day' every two weeks (change the frequency according to the L2 schedule and the needs or interests of the children). On that day each of them will bring paper for letters and an envelope.

In class

1. Write on the blackboard:

    Dear Friend

    Let the children copy it on their papers. Then ask the children what they want
    to write in the message or letter. Elicit ideas from them and write these ideas
    on the blackboard. The children follow your model and write the same expressions
    on their papers, following a kind of group letter format. However, each child
    uses his own personal information. Go around, check what the children have written
    and give extra help.

2. Write the names of the children who will receive the letters on the blackboard.
    Ask your children to put the letters in the envelope, select one name and write
    it on the envelope. Make sure that every child in the other class will receive a
    letter. Collect the letters.

3. At the end of class bring the letters to the other children. In a similar session
    they read their letters and answer them. This mail will continue as long as the
    children have an interest in keeping it going. This will prepare them for future
    pen-friends living abroad.

    Have this group letter when the children are beginning their letter-writing
    instruction.

Variations

Make it difficult

At later stages, encourage the children to work individually. The content of the message
or letter is determined by how much L2 the children have acquired and by the set
of communicative functions the children have been exposed to. However, some suitable
themes may be the following:

- Introduce yourself.
- Give personal information.
- Talk about your family.
- Talk about your favourite toys or sports.
- Invite your friend to a 'sandwich together' during the break.
- Invite your friend to go back home with you.
- Invite your friend to take the school bus with you.
- Invite your friend to come to your home in the afternoon to play.
- Inform your friend about the basketball class schedule.
- Invite your friend to join the basketball class.
- Invite your friend to your birthday party, give the date, the time, the address,
  and the telephone number.

Obviously, select or change the themes according to the reality in which the children live. Letters and messages do not necessarily have to be long. Even one sentence (message) or one paragraph (letter) may be enough at the beginning of this letter-writing instruction.

Links

You may link this activity with: **Show and tell (14)**; **Be mine ... on Valentine's Day (87)**.

Teacher's diary

Are your children ready for letter writing? Have they asked you how to do it? Do they enjoy the group letter phase? Do they help each other? How often do you think your students need to do letter writing to reach basic competence in it? How long will they need?

87   Be mine . . . on Valentine's Day

Topic	Valentine's cards, affection
Activity type	Writing
Language	Focus on the language of messages
Background knowledge	The children should have basic skills in reading and writing
Time	30—50 minutes
Classroom setting	Any
Materials	A list of Valentine's expressions; a set of cards; a shoe box for each child
Age	7 and above
Level	Elementary and above, depending on the difficulty of the messages
Purpose	Increasing the children's ability to communicate via messages

Preparation

Collect as many shoe boxes as the number of children in class and bring them to school. Bring also a set of cards suitable for Valentine's Day.

In class

1. Make a rectangular hole in each box. The children help you. Then they write their names on their boxes. Put the boxes on a table.

2. Explain to the children what Valentine's Day is. Tell them that in many schools children exchange cards on this particular day to show affection.

3. Ask the children what expressions they would like to write to a good friend. Elicit short expressions in the L1. Translate these expressions into the L2 and write them at random on the blackboard. Add other expressions that you have selected for this activity.

4. Ask the children to read the expressions aloud. Ask which ones they like best and why.

5. Ask the children to get the cards. Now the 'card writing' begins. Tell them to follow these steps for each card:

   • Write the name of the friend at the top of the card.

   • Select an expression from the blackboard.

   • Copy it onto the card.

   • Decorate the card with a drawing.

   • Sign it.

   When all the cards are ready, they go to the table and put the cards into the boxes of the children they are sending the cards to. While the children are doing this, go around the desks and give help.

6. The children open the boxes and read the cards that they have received, show them to their peers and read the messages aloud.
   The following are expressions that you may use for this activity:

   Be my Valentine.
   I'm all yours, Valentine!
   You're totally wonderful!
   Between you and me, there is perfect harmony.
   Won't you be mine?
   Happy Valentine's Day.
   Hoping you'll be mine.
   Hi Valentine! Be mine!
   You walked right into my heart!
   You make me feel like dancing.
   Just a little note to say 'Happy Valentine's Day!'
   You're my favourite!
   You look marvellous, Valentine.
   You're a real Valentine.
   For a sweet friend.

You're all 'heart'.
Stop and be mine, Valentine.
Know why I'm sending this Valentine? To tell you I'm glad you're a friend of mine.
Glad I discovered you, Valentine.

Variations

The children prepare their own Valentine's cards.

Links

You may link this activity with: **Your 'closest' pen-friend (86)**.

Teacher's diary

Was it complicated for you to organise this activity? If yes, how can you make the preparation more simple? Did the children enjoy writing and receiving cards? How much language will they retain from this experience?

SECTION VI

TIME FOR REWARDS

Use this section as a source for rewards to give to the children any time you feel they need one or when you check their folders. Make photocopies* of the pages. Cut out the rewards. Select the ones you want to give to the children and stick them in their folders.

REWARDS

*You are permitted to photocopy these pages for classroom use.

 GOOD JOB

 NOT YET! TRY AGAIN

 YOU DID A GREAT JOB TODAY!!

WONDERFUL

F A N
TAST
I C

 DON'T be messy!

Today, you've been very good at
— — — — — — — — — — — — — —

TODAY, you've been good at:
☐ drawing   ☐ reading
☐ speaking ☐ writing
☐ listening ☐ helping your class- mates
☐ doing groupwork

CONGRATULATIONS!
You've been good at
— — — — — — — —

INDEXES

A. Index of activities by type

This section indicates the major action performed by the children within the activities. In all the activities, however, the children perform other actions as well.

Art

The hungriest poster (117)
Colour game: primary and
  secondary colours (119)

Building up sentences

The ball (21)
The 'what, when, where, how'
  game (174)

Building up stories

Jigsaw story (176)
Your story, my writing (190)

Class routines

Date, weather, time, the register
  (95)
Extra cards? Put them in the
  pocket (113)
Instructions (99)
Make your own calendar (96)
The classroom dictionary (115)
The dictionary poster (109)
The 'ME' sign-board (35)

Counting

Blind steps (151)
1–2–3–4 ... FREEZE! (88)
Inventory (147)

Describing

The 'ME' poster (131)
The touch and feel book: make
  your own (126)

Evaluating the work done

If walls talk you read them (186)
Show me your folder (201)

Expressing opinions

Footcolour (123)

Language play

I say, you repeat (59)
Nonsense language (51)
Sounds (55)
The funny answer (53)
The onomatopoeic game (57)

Learning about foreign cultures

Getting ready for 'A day in the
  life of ... (153)
Halloween (157)
Races (43)

Learning and recognising words

Colour game: primary and
  secondary colours (119)
Class labels (170)
Closer — closer (81)
Compound words (166)
Extra cards? Put them in the
  pocket (113)
Families (40)
1–2–3–4 ... FREEZE! (88)
If I ... (111)
Let's pretend we are animals
  (76)
Listen and draw (121)
L2 'borrowing game' (61)
Paper-bag faces (83)
Picture compound words (163)
Races (43)
Rap the words (133)
Replay (17)
Search for the English word (143)
Shape in, shape out (145)
Stop when you hear ... (19)
The classroom band (135)

The classroom dictionary (115)
The hungriest poster (117)
What's missing? (86)
Words in sight (168)

Listening to a story

A noisy story, a noisy picture
  (192)
A quiet story, a quiet picture
  (194)
Look, listen and move (139)
Shall we read a fairy-tale? (196)
Your story, my writing (190)

Making reports

Book 'n' balloons (188)
If walls talk you read them (186)
Inventory (147)
Let's measure up our classroom
  (149)

Playing fantasy games

Our little people (70)

Playing 'let's pretend'

A day in the life of ... (155)
Let's pretend we are animals
  (76)
Let's pretend we are weather
  forecasters (74)

Playing realistic games

The micro-cities (72)

Playing with the alphabet

Alphabet line (105)
Letter shape (103)
The 'moving letter' (101)

B. Index of activities by school subject

Here are listed those activities that have a specific link with subjects in the curriculum. Many other activities in the book can be related to these subjects, although they do not have such a specific link as the ones listed below.

Art

Colour game: primary and
  secondary colours (119)
Footcolour (123)
Listen and draw (121)
Shall we read a fairy-tale? (196)
The hungriest poster (117)
The 'ME' poster (131)
The touch and feel book: make
  your own (126)

Culture

A day in the life of ... (155)
Getting ready for 'A day in the
  life of ...' (153)
Halloween (157)
Races (43)

Maths

Blind steps (157)
Inventory (147)

Let's measure up our classroom
  (149)

Music

Rap the words (133)
The classroom band (135)

Physical Education

Body movements (137)
Look, listen and move (139)
Search for the English word (143)
Shape in, shape out (145)

C. Index of activities by proficiency level

Most of the following activities can be adapted at different proficiency levels (elementary, intermediate and advanced), depending on the materials used and on the result that you want to achieve.

Beginning students

Chase and catch (79)
Class labels (170)
Closer — closer (81)
Follow the leader (28)
1–2–3–4 ... FREEZE! (88)
Letter shape (103)
L2 'borrowing' game (61)
Name cards (34)
Nonsense language (51)
Rap the words (133)
Replay (17)
Ring-a-ring-a-rosy (32)
Rush the sentence (23)
Sounds (55)
The ball (21)
The crazy train (30)
The funny answer (53)
The 'ME' sign-board (35)
The 'moving letter' (101)

Elementary students

A birthday gift (108)
A day in the life of ... (155)
Alphabet line (105)
Be mine ... on Valentine's Day (213)
Blind steps (151)
Body movements (137)
Book 'n' balloons (188)
Bubbles search (184)
Chase and catch (79)
Choose the punctuation (205)
Classdance (141)
Closer — closer (81)
Colour game: primary and secondary colours (119)

Date, weather, time, the register (95)
Extra cards? Put them in the pocket (113)
Families (40)
First day at school (63)
Follow the leader (28)
Footcolour (123)
1–2–3–4 ... FREEZE! (88)
Gestures (25)
Getting ready for 'A day in the life of ...' (153)
Halloween (157)
Hopscotch (90)
I say, you repeat (59)
If I ... (111)
If walls talk you read them (186)
Instructions (99)
Inventory (147)
Let's measure up our classroom (149)
Let's pretend we are animals (76)
Let's pretend we are weather forecasters (74)
Letter shape (103)
Listen and draw (121)
Look, listen and move (139)
L2 'borrowing' game (61)
Make a poem (207)
Make your own calendar (96)
Name cards (34)
Our little people (70)
Paper-bag faces (83)
Picture compound words (163)
Races (43)
Read 'n' shout (178)
Runaway capitals (203)

Rush the sentence (23)
Search for the English word (143)
Shall we read a fairy-tale? (196)
Shape in, shape out (145)
Show and tell (45)
Show me your folder (201)
Stop when you hear ... (19)
The ball (21)
The classroom band (135)
The classroom dictionary (115)
The crazy train (30)
The dictionary poster (109)
The hungriest poster (117)
The 'ME' poster (131)
The micro-cities (72)
The 'moving letter' (101)
The onomatopoeic game (57)
The 'what, when, where, how' game (174)
What's missing? (86)
Who's got the ring? (47)
Words in sight (168)

Intermediate students

A birthday gift (108)
A day in the life of ... (155)
Be mine ... on Valentine's Day (213)
Body movements (137)
Book 'n' balloons (188)
Bubbles search (184)
Choose what to say (172)
Classdance (141)
Compound words (166)
Extra cards? Put them in the pocket (113)
First day at school (63)